FIFTIES STYLE

Then and Now

FIFTIES STYLE

Then and Now

By
Richard Horn

COLUMBUS
BOOKS

A FRIEDMAN GROUP BOOK

Published by Columbus Books,
19–23 Ludgate Hill
London, EC4M 7PD

ISBN: 0-86287-081-X
ISBN: 0-86287-086-0 (paperback)

FIFTIES STYLE: Then and Now
was prepared and produced by
Michael Friedman Publishing Group, Inc.
15 West 26th Street
New York, N.Y. 10010

Editor: Naomi Black
Art Director: Richard Boddy
Designer: Mary Moriarty
Photo Editor: Susan M. Duane

Typeset by BPE Graphics, Inc.
Color separations by Hong Kong Scanner Craft Company Ltd.
Printed and bound in Hong Kong by Leefung-Asco Printers Ltd.

Reprinted 1987

Dedication

For Edgardo

Acknowledgments

Many people provided me with invaluable help in the course of my putting together this book—too many to name at one go. However, I do want to thank Ralph Cutler, Mark Isaacson, and Mark McDonald of Fifty/50 in New York City for their time and generosity. On the West Coast, photographer Tim Street-Porter and architect Alan Hess were both wonderfully supportive and inspiring. In New York, Mark and Melody Bennett, fifties addicts if ever there were ones, were kindred spirits full of boundless enthusiasm and humor. The time I spent talking with designers Vladimir Kagan, Erwine Laverne, John van Kort, and Edward Wormley brought the 1950s design scene alive for me in a way no amount of research could have.

At Quarto, Naomi Black was the most patient and resourceful editor a writer could hope for, gifted with the skills of a mind reader and the voice of reason. Fearless picture researcher Susan Duane fulfilled a harrowing assignment with brilliance, persistence, and admirable optimism: that is, the task of getting hold of this book's illustrations, a tracking down that would have driven the most determined sleuth to despair. Thanks also go to Marta Hallett for her sense of diplomacy and equally welcome sense of the absurd.

I also thank Mary Moriarty, FIFTIES STYLE's graphic designer, for her consistently witty and intelligent responses to the countless demands a book of this nature (and an author of this nature) are bound to make.

In addition, I want to express my gratitude to Stanley Coren of Beige, in New York City. Quick-witted and unencumbered by received ideas, he would listen to my crazy speculations, spur me on with equally crazy but lucid and on-target speculations of his own, and help me grasp what strength lay in doubting and what fun in seeing over, under, and through the surface of things.

I would also like to express my gratitude to Peter Lemos for his deft solution to an irksome problem. Susan Harkavy of the American Craft Museum was very helpful in the early stages of this project. Tracey Harden, Cynthia Hill, and Jim Kemp provided excellent ''eighties-style'' sounding boards for some of my ideas. My deepest thanks go and continue to go to Billy Bergman, Gail Kinn, and Dr. Rachel Trubowitz for their unflagging patience, optimism, encouragement, and humor.

Contents

Introduction

It is the eighties, but the fifties live again. Postwar furniture, the latest and hottest entry into the antiques market, is quickly snapped up by private collectors and museums on both sides of the Atlantic. Movies and plays set in the 1950s continue to attract crowds. Many of today's magazines, record albums, and advertisements offer stylish updates of fifties graphics. America's postmodern architects and Europe's furniture designers (especially those involved with the Memphis design movement) draw upon the rich multiplicity of the buildings and objects of that period, while *haute couture* and New Wave street fashion alike appropriate fifties motifs, swiftly translating them into an eighties sensibility.

The part nostalgia plays in all this is obvious enough. We miss the innocent fifties—and forget the Cold War tensions, H-bomb anxieties, shortages, and postwar reconstruction. When we think of the 1950s, we think not of these drearier facets but of a more positive side—the economic ''miracles'' of those years, which saw the blossoming of a full-blown consumer culture in Western Europe that rivalled that of the United States. This heady, nearly ten-year-long shopping spree, this unabashedly hedonistic orgy of acquiring—this we look back on with affection and, given the awful trials of World War II, tolerance. And it is this consumerism, this frank acknowledgement of robust appetites, that made fifties design possible.

The idea of a ''fifties style'' is, in many ways, misleading. More accurate would be ''fifties style*s*.'' For European design of the 1950s, as well as the American design which influenced it and which it influenced in turn, featured not one look but many. This is true not only of fashion, where mercurial style-changes are the norm, but of all aspects of design. The 1950s are said to have witnessed the triumph of Modern design in Europe and America. In fact, it was not so much Modern design—that is, a distinct style in and of itself, Bauhaus-influenced, and concerned with simple forms and technological innovations—that prevailed; it was the very notion (or notions) of and the rigorous questioning or vigorous acceptance of *modernity* itself. With World War II over, Europeans felt ready to begin anew. The past was past. Designers, along with everyone else, trained their gazes on the promising future. But not all of Europe's fifties designers regarded that future from the same perspective. Taking—at least in part—their cue from the American designers whose work is highlighted in this book, some were wildly optimistic—and that optimism comes through in their work. Others exercised caution—a caution expressed in rather conservative, though at the same time fresh-looking, designs. Then there were men and women who took a more pragmatic approach and created highly practical, rather unemotional designs. It is this multiplicity of approaches that informs the design of the 1950s. And it is this multiplicity that I have tried to convey in this book. All of these approaches can be seen as interesting responses to the modern, postwar age: I choose not to say which responses were aesthetically, functionally, and/or commercially valid and which were not; I only hope to show as much as possible and give some idea of the amazingly rich, varied, and often beautiful American designs of those years—designs that have fascinated Europeans and Americans.

The chapters of this book present various aspects of the American design of the 1950s that, to a greater or lesser extent, influenced European design—products, graphics, craft objects, furniture and furnishings, interiors, architecture, and fashion. Each chapter also includes photographic examples of work by designers and artists of the 1980s that show a marked fifties influence or that offer reinterpretations of one of the various styles current at that time. Finally, a source list is provided, for those who wish to acquire these eighties updates or the boldly imaginative originals that characterized one of the most imaginative and exuberant, if sometimes misguided, chapters of twentieth-century design history.

Bob Murray

1
Product Design

Postwar Americans demanded a host of new design "looks" to reflect and enhance their optimistic mood and erase memories of deprivation due to wartime shortages. Furniture, graphic, product, and fashion designers all responded accordingly. But perhaps no designers met those demands as completely as those who designed America's cars. Big, long, bulky, low-slung, colorful, sleekly curvaceous, and gleaming with ornamental chrome, fifties cars were exuberant creations, rivaled only by the decade's way-out

Cruisin'

free-form furniture and roadside architecture and perhaps some of the more extravagantly exotic women's evening wear. While Modernist tenets favoring functionality, subdued colors, and simple, unornamented forms held sway in many areas of fifties design, they went unheeded by the design departments of General Motors, Chrysler, and Ford. Year after year, under the directorship of Harley J. Earl at General Motors, Virgil Exner at Chrysler, and George Walker at Ford, these companies turned out designs that were outrageous essays in pure style, visual odes to American ideals of power, mobility, and speed.

The cars of the fifties were graced with spacious interiors that made long trips as comfortable as possible. Furthermore, they boasted welcome conveniences such as high-performance engines, better brake and lighting systems, and automatic transmissions. Basically, though, the cars were thoroughly impractical. They guzzled gas. Their functional deficiencies were no secret, nor was their "planned obsolescence"—that is, the fact that the cars were built not to last but to become unfashionable and nonfunc-

tional so quickly that in a matter of (ideally) one or two years' time an owner would be obliged to get rid of whichever car he or she had and buy a new one. The size of these massive vehicles made them hard to park, especially in cities. And because there were so many of them—by 1954 there were forty-seven million passenger cars registered in the United States and by 1960 four-fifths of all American families owned cars—they tended to clog up in traffic jams. The overcrowding continued even with the 41,000

miles of wide new roads built in accordance with the 1956 Interstate Highway Act.

These drawbacks bothered no one. Americans in the fifties did not care much about a car's practicality. What appealed to them most was its value as a symbol of both status and power. This was particularly true in the suburbs, where cars were essential not only to daily living but to the new, shared belief in conspicuous consumption that bound the inhabitants of these nonethnic anti-neighborhoods together. In fact, the fetishistic quality of these idols-on-wheels was most obvious, with their cruel-looking tail fins, grinning front grilles, tensed wraparound windshields, and splendid bodies lashed with chrome highlights. Thanks in part to a relentless advertising push and in part to people's imaginations, the different models of cars, like the gods and goddesses of some polytheistic religion, took on personalities of their own, so that driving this or that model seemed to tell much about the person who drove it. This bizarre deification became most pronounced with the blossoming of teenage car culture in the mid-1950s, when cus-

Sleek monsters like this one looked better on the open road than in the traffic jams they helped create on city streets unprepared for the fifties' car invasion.

Sexy car. Sexy boy. Rocket car. All seem genealogically linked in this painting by young artworld superstar Kenny Scharf, done in 1979.

tomization made the autos look more zoomorphic than ever.

If Americans did not exactly worship their cars, they did see them as being endowed, in a certain sense, with quasi-supernatural powers. Eric Larrabee, for one, detected a magical quality in the baroque excesses of fifties automobiles when he wrote that "the car is an instrument against the very *idea* of chores and inconveniences, regardless of their reality. To be splendid and irrational is of its na-

ture." Indeed, no object embodies the unreality of the fifties so well as the automobiles manufactured during those years. While rationality figured prominently in other areas of fifties life (witness the decade's logically—if insensitively—planned suburban communities, the proliferation of corporate hierarchies, the emotional blankness of the proverbial man in the gray flannel suit, as well as the prevalent social conformism), cars were intended as fantasies, sold as fantasies, and

bought, in part, as fantasies. The late 1950s economic slump and the launching of *Sputnik* by America's archenemy, Russia, provided a double dose of reality. But for the years during which Americans could afford to avoid reality, forget about space races and financial woes, and go through life as if it were one big, open road leading toward a wonderful future, no vehicle could have been more appropriate for the journey than the now-classic 1950s automobile.

Courtesy of the artist Mark Bennett

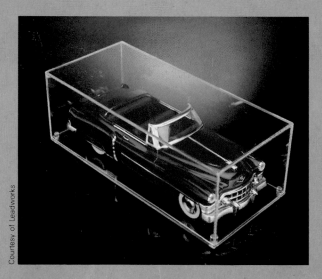

Courtesy of Leadworks

This see-through eighties sarcophagus for a miniature 1950s Cadillac is from Leadworks in Beachwood, Ohio.

Convertibles like the 1959 model depicted in this 1978 collage drawing by Mark Bennett were owned by fast-lane types who liked to have a good time by driving around with the top down, to achieve that quintessentially American experience of plowing down a sunlit interstate with the wind blowing through one's hair. Compared to those on the Caddys, these fins are rather modest. Note the chrome detailing though—that important selling point for automobile manufacturers back in the fifties.

"What's good for the country is good for General Motors, and what's good for General Motors is good for the country," said Charles E. Wilson, Secretary of Defense under President Eisenhower and former president of the company that manufactured this sensible-looking Chevrolet Bel Air. The car may call up all sorts of nostalgic reveries. The sentiment, in a way, sounds curiously contemporary.

During the 1950s, America became a nation of consumers—literally and figuratively. Oral cravings ran high. Gourmet cooking began to attract more adherents, thanks partly to the burgeoning do-it-yourself movement and partly to the increasing global awareness brought about by the mass media and, later in the decade, jet travel. What's more, with the emphasis on family "togetherness" and obligatory sociability—both effective antidotes to the harrowing discontinuities and personal losses experienced during the

low, and the newly popular copper, along with the customary white. The overall effect of these pieces was sleek and not a little antiseptic—which is to say stylish, as far as 1950s America was concerned.

Quite apart from their clean-lined styling, many of these appliances were far more convenient than earlier models. There was more storage space in refrigerators, more practical positioning of controls on ranges, and several cycles for dishwashers. Numerous electrically powered smaller

What's Cooking?

war—the kitchen became, once again, an important room in the house.

"Dream kitchens" of the fifties were billed as gleaming models of efficiency. There, each cabinet and appliance had its proper place—an idyllic picture, completed by the fifties housewife, whose place, by choice, this kitchen was. With an eye on the trend toward pared-down Modern design, manufacturers stopped producing the bulbous refrigerators, toasters, ranges, and so on that were holdovers from the pre-World War II years. Shifting gears, they began to offer rigidly rectilinear appliances with a minimum of hardware. These, if not actually built in, would have the sort of built-in—or, in the lingo of the day, "architectural"—appearance previously affordable only by the rich. However, while Modernist designers and architects eschewed most color, appliance manufacturers embraced it, offering suites of appliances in matching hues, such as cerulean blue, sea green, yel-

items such as can openers and egg beaters also made life easier. What's more, appliance parts became increasingly standardized, so that production costs were cut and items priced more affordably. Still, as in the auto industry, the obligatory new models came out yearly, many of them featuring superficial improvements such as chrome trim on refrigerators and complicated-looking, color-coded control panels on stoves, the one recalling automobile ornaments, the other a car's dashboard.

Like appliances, cookware enjoyed a healthy boom during the 1950s. Diversified implements abounded, from rotisseries and barbecues to new lines of oven-to-table ware to the usual pots and pans. Whether it was made of aluminum, copper, steel, wood, plastic, glass, or straw, the typical piece of fifties cookware had a simple, no-nonsense form. Its designer would have meant it to be functional first. Its "honest" good looks were conveyed

Fifties tableware, quirkily shaped and bizarrely patterned, can lend a note of levity to casual dinners with friends. *California Mobile,* from the Poppytrail line by Metlox, a California manufacturer, was produced during the latter half of the 1950s and can now be found at New York's Beige Gallery. Its squiggle designs (shades of Kandinsky and Miró) and boomeranging forms have resurfaced in—and are bound to appeal to those with a taste for—today's New Wave style.

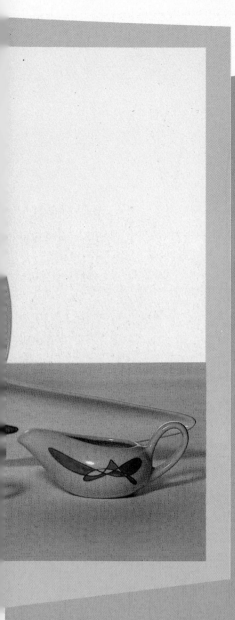

Courtesy of the designer George Nelson

he winter 1951–52 issue of the *Everyday Art Quarterly* (now known as *Design Quarterly*) offered the following guidelines for dinnerware. It should be ''1. *simple.* It is background for food. 2. *easy to handle.* Because it is almost more handled than looked at, it should be a. light in weight b. easily stacked c. easily cleaned. 3. as nearly *expendable* as possible.'' The ''Florence Ware'' service, designed in 1955 for Prolon by Irving Harper of George Nelson Associates and made of durable melamine, meets those guidelines with inventiveness and flair.

This pure, almost Japanese-looking dinnerware has not become dated at all and would work well with today's ''lifestyle'' furniture, stemware, and flatware.

hanks to such then-new techniques as oiling, buffing, scratchbrushing, satin finishing and coloring, 1950s aluminum products like these serving pieces from the Beige Gallery took on an attractiveness and variety that met the demands of novelty-hungry consumers.

Coloring aluminum masked its industrial quality, and made it more appealing to homemakers. The rich, metallic hues characteristic of colored aluminum can still be seen in products manufactured today.

Michael Zapatello. Courtesy of Beige Gallery

Courtesy of Tupperware

Developed in the early forties, flexible, translucent, plastic Tupperware, created by Earl Tupper, first achieved popularity in the early 1950s. Airtight, waterproof, and available in a spectrum of pastel hues, it is still widely used today.

by sensible proportions, clean lines, and on occasion, a subtle juxtaposing of materials that, if not exactly satisfying people's supposed craving for ornament, did create a degree of visual interest.

During the 1950s, revolutionary developments occurred in tableware as well, with melamine—an inexpensive, lightweight plastic—playing a leading role and other types of plastic and aluminum taking featured parts. At first people shunned plastic, dismissing it as overly cheap-, institutional-,

and/or disposable-looking; the 1950s, however, ushered in the widespread use of disposable plastic plates, containers, and other throwaway items. And when sophisticated designers such as George Nelson and Russel Wright tried their hands at creating lines of plastic dinnerware, the simple, elegant, rather Japanese-looking results won high praise. Other plastics were used to create a variety of serving and storage pieces, of which the most notable was the enormously successful Tupperware, made of molded poly-

ethylene. At the same time, sturdy and equally simple ceramic ware was also produced.

The decade's glassware and flatware—much of it eminently affordable and widely available—were also characterized by simple, unornamented forms. Indeed, if Modernism triumphed in any one area of design, it was in the field of fifties tableware. While gaudier, futuristic designs did exist, the practicality and simplicity of some of the other pieces proved irresistible to many.

Mark and Melody Bennett, who are avid collectors of American fifties designs, have furnished the kitchen of their New York City apartment entirely with 1950s pieces. The table and chairs are by Paul McCobb. *Talk of the Town* Melmac tableware (from Harmony House) on the table includes squarish plates that were quite popular during the fifties. The room itself seems to exist in a time warp, as if the fifties had never ended—an impression enhanced by the fact that, out the window, one sees nothing but buildings built before 1959. Below, pastel-toned kitchen appliances like this refrigerator sold well during the 1950s, and can still do the decorating trick in an eighties kitchen. Colors like this pretty pink were decided upon by manufacturers as an important selling point.

Bob Murray

Richard Ross

Amateur photography first became a popular pastime in the fifties. However, it took some time for camera manufacturers to give their products an appropriately "fifties" look. These early 1950s Kodaks, for example, still feature the streamlining and rounded-off corners associated with the style that had just passed—forties Moderne. These cameras *have* a style because miniaturization opened up new horizons after World War II. Because a camera's inner mechanisms were too small to greatly affect its appearance, the designer was free to give it a stylish look that had little to do with its workings.

Taking It Easy

Shorter working hours, more efficient machinery, factories closed on Saturdays, and higher salaries all gave fifties Americans amounts of leisure time formerly unheard of for all but the wealthy. As one writer put it in a 1954 issue of *Industrial Design*, "Today's average American, with so much time on his hands and so little to escape from, almost inevitably turns to recreation of a wholesome and purposeful flavor, whether it be sports, culture, or family life." Naturally, America's entrepreneurially minded were quick to make the most of this situation. Boating, bowling, amateur photography, audiophile pursuits, travel—once the chosen, affordable activities became available, they provided a way of filling spare time that was both pleasurable to the consumer and financially remunerative to the manufacturer.

The design of these objects, at least in terms of styling, tended to be unexceptional. True, outboard motors, luggage, and bowling equipment often did assume a strikingly sculptural appearance. But for the most part, it was

John Heskett, in his book *Industrial Design*, discusses the American penchant for taking to the water. By 1959 seven million Americans owned boats, many like the one shown here, with an outboard motor designed by Brooks Stevens for Evinrude, a division of the Outboard Marine Corporation.

the "gadget" aspect that was emphasized. Form followed function; indeed, the more complicated the technological (as opposed to "packaged") look of an object, the greater seemed both its novelty and its promise of modern wonders hitherto unknown to man. Of course, in the interest of selling as many commodities to as many people as possible, manufacturers made sure that these gadgets—whether they were tape recorders, hi-fis, or cameras—were easy to operate.

But, of course, the most popular means of relaxing during the 1950s was with television. In 1950 three million Americans owned television sets. By the end of the decade, the number rose to fifty million. The early televisions were unstylishly bulky and reception was poor. But as technology developed, the tube grew larger, and both picture quality and styling improved. The main debate regarding the television set as an *object*—as opposed to a new medium—revolved around the issue of whether it was to be treated as a piece of furniture or as a technological instrument whose functional aspect should by no means be hidden. Television cabinets of the decade were usually made of wood, had a sleek, rectilinear appearance, and often stood—like so much fifties furniture—several inches off the ground on splayed, turned legs. Thus, this alien object could be easily assimilated into the decorative scheme of any room. Given the propensity of Americans in the fifties for turning television-watching into a social occasion, the set sometimes became the central piece of furniture in the room, especially when it was dolled up with a slipcover and topped with one of the decade's myriad television lamps— lamps made specifically to be put on top of an unbecomingly bare television set. Only the tube posed a problem. When not receiving, it became a bizarre, ever-present, staring eye—a disturbing feature remedied by sliding panels and tambour doors that hid the tube from view when not in use.

The more futuristic-looking television sets, while often striking, did not attract as wide a public as the more unobtrusive pieces. It was only when smaller, lightweight, portable televisions started to be manufactured in the mid-1950s that people accepted— and bought—sets that looked not like pieces of furniture but like somewhat organic plastic objects, with handles rounded for easier gripping and edges rounded in part for safety's sake, in part for the sake of appearance. By that time, it was not uncommon for a household to have more than one television, a phenomenon that continues to this day and will most likely continue into the future.

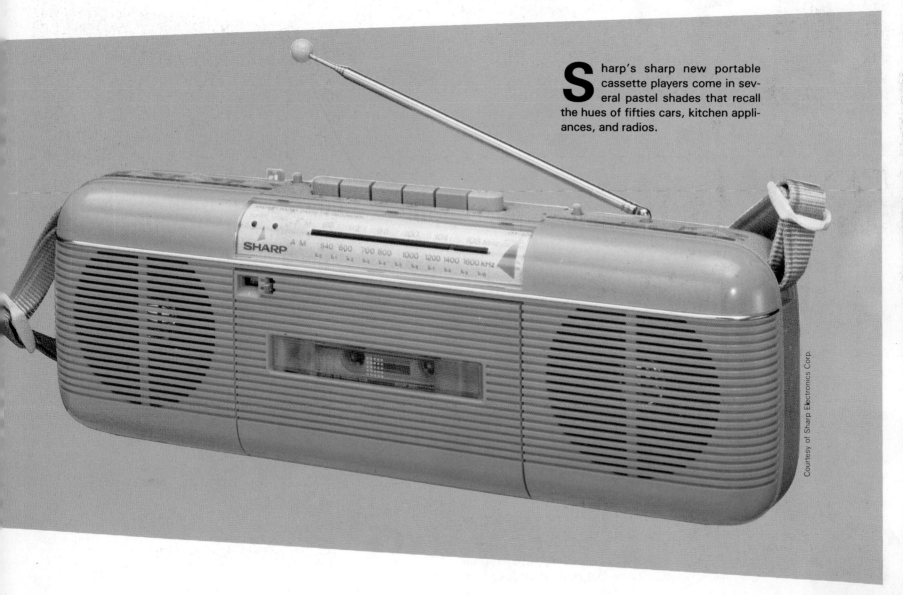

Sharp's sharp new portable cassette players come in several pastel shades that recall the hues of fifties cars, kitchen appliances, and radios.

Courtesy of Sharp Electronics Corp.

Art by Jim Heimann

n Jim Heimann's recent illustration *(left)*, the fifties television is endowed with total recall of the most potent imagery of that decade. All the channels play at once, making for some not-so-homey clutter.

By the end of the fifties *(above)*, television's hypnotic hold over Americans had become unbreakable.

The table model of Philco's 1958 Predicta line of television sets featured a swiveling screen. Its unusual shape did not endear it to many consumers. Today, however, it is considered a prized collectors' item that, as it happens, still works remarkably well.

Like their parents, the 1950s boom babies liked to have fun. Toy manufacturers responded accordingly. If there was one substance that enabled manufacturers to materialize that response, it was plastic. Frisbees and hula hoops, the vast array of model kits that became available during this do-it-yourself decade, toy robots, those curiously fascinating pieces of inorganic matter known as Play-Doh and Silly Putty, Barbie and Ken dolls—all were made of one or another type of plastic. And while, as Inez and Marshall Mc-

Clintock assert in *Toys in America,* children's perennial favorites—dolls, guns, trains, balls, bikes, miniature cars, and games—remained the same during the fifties, versatile plastic held out the promise of new and unlimited possibilities for the imaginative toy designer and equally unlimited sales potential for his employer.

If plastic items seemed to glut the toy market, there was room for more sophisticated playthings as well. These colorful and often rather abstract Modern objects were meant to delight par-

Playtime

Charles and Ray Eames created this *Little Toy* in 1951.

These days, Mattel's Barbie *(left)* might be seen on beaches in somewhat more risqué attire, but her popularity is every bit as strong now as it was in the fifties. Back then, the doll could "pose as if running, cheerleading or modeling," as an ad had it. When not engaged in any of these activities, Barbie always had her "dreamy date," Ken, he of the "manly physique...molded of sturdy plastic," for companionship. Today, as Mattel's current licensing director Bev Cannaday notes, "Barbie is very much in tune with the modern girl. Whatever the current fashion, it's incorporated into the Barbie collection."

This unusual couple *(right)*—Mr. and Mrs. Potato Head—is still on the market today. The originals, however, can be bought in some specialty toy shops.

Courtesy of Hasbro Ind. Inc.

ents as much as children, and they were sold in the sort of specialty shops frequented by those with an eye for what the Museum of Modern Art termed "Good Design." Some imaginatively conceived playground equipment was also available, much of it featuring the biomorphic forms that were popular in so many different areas of 1950s design.

Although the more sophisticated playthings expressed a designer's individual touch, the designs of most mass-marketed toys of the 1950s grew not so much out of an individual's outlook as from the results of extensive market research. Manufacturers consulted educators, salespeople, and child psychologists before investing in a product. This care led to toys that were fun for a child to play with *and* instrumental in helping him or her acquire manual skills. Yet many of the toys had a noticeable blandness to them, almost as if they were designed by committee rather than by a single person—a blandness that smacked of commercialism and considerations of the bottom line. However, given the increasing homogenization of American life in the 1950s, the blurring of class and ethnic distinctions, and the twin, equally indiscriminate orgies of postwar marketing and acquiring, this blandness must be seen, in retrospect, as nothing but appropriate. Indeed, one is almost tempted to call those bland toys more characteristically American—perhaps even more beautiful—than the decade's self-consciously well-designed "designer" toys.

GIRDER & PANEL BIG CITY SET

Courtesy of Kenner (Girder and Panel® building set)

Budding young architects may have developed their skills in the fifties with Kenner's Girder & Panel set and Action building set. Postmodernist architecture notwithstanding, similar toys today still employ Modernism's vocabulary.

Bob Murray

This Howdy Doody puppet is as entertaining today as it was thirty years ago. What kid, even in the jaded eighties, could resist?

Bob Murray

New techniques for coloring aluminum, developed in the 1950s, helped foster Slinky in a variety of metallic hues. This simple, clever toy design continues to fascinate children even in our hyper-advanced era. Eighties versions are available in a still wider variety of bright colors and sizes.

It may have been true that Americans of the fifties found little in the world to escape from. Given their country's power abroad and racial segregation at home, it was easy for people—particularly the middle-class, white suburbanites who, thanks to the generalizations of the mass media, emerged as the decade's prototypical Americans—to ignore the world's complexities and go on leading the good life. Bearing in mind the country's puritan roots, however, it is not altogether surprising that during the

responsibilities, such as caring for the children and taking part in community activities.

The men of the pre-househusband era were employed not at home but at a factory or office. And yet they, too, found work to do around the house in their spare time. Indeed, many men felt that they *needed* such work, deprived as they were of the invigorating physicality of manual labor by this push-button, automated world. That deprivation provoked a minor counterrevolution: the do-it-yourself move-

Homework

1950s "the good life" encompassed not only relaxing at home but working there, too.

Housewives, of course, *had* to do housework. Popular wisdom held that those who eschewed carpet sweepers, vacuum cleaners, and mops were excessively neurotic, too manly, or lesbian—dire verdicts in a rigidly conformist, sexually repressed decade. Manufacturers flooded the market with countless items suitable for all household chores. These were not only functional and convenient but decorative, too, in an understated, elegant way, so as to give housework the brisk, compelling quality all the ads said it had. Made of plastics or metals capable of being colored and textured in a variety of ways, they injected (usually pastel) brightness, if not into the harried homemaker's life, then at least into whichever room she happened to be cleaning. In both styling and practicality, these items were a vast improvement on similar objects used before World War II, which tended to be clumsy, cumbersome, and drab-looking. What's more, their easy-to-use, labor-saving qualities allowed women more time to see to their other

ment. Nowhere was this movement more evident than in the field of home improvements and repairs—a field that, given the shoddy construction of postwar suburban homes, was wide open in the fifties. A man may have seen himself as a "pencil-pushing" automaton in a vast hierarchy at the office or as a replaceable part at the factory. At home, though, with the easy-to-use, portable, and handsome-looking power hand tools that became widely available in the 1950s, he could spend his leisure time in a purposeful, physically-demanding project that he initiated and completed.

It is interesting to note that, while the curving, molded contours of these tools resembled those of the household cleaning implements, their colors were usually much bolder. This is a clear instance of how, through something as seemingly neutral as product design, the rigid sexual distinction between males and females that prevailed throughout the 1950s was emphasized. And one should not be taken in by the few pastel-toned tools of the decade: these were aimed not at Rosie the Riveter but at the woman out buying a gift for her husband.

In David Sandlin's 1984 drawing entitled *Backyard of Earthly Delights,* a fifties housewife goes about her household chores with all the glee, grace, and "creativity" the magazines of that period recommended.

During the fifties, the suburban population included countless Mr. Fix-Its. With the boom of the do-it-yourself era, what better way to sell a product than by picturing it with the home tool kit?

Courtesy of Whirlpool Corp.

Whirlpool washing machines of the early 1950s still had some of the streamline contouring that characterized models of the forties. The boxy, architectural look of late fifties washers and driers has gone more or less unaltered to the present, despite the many space-saving features appliance manufacturers now bestow on these products.

This Means Business

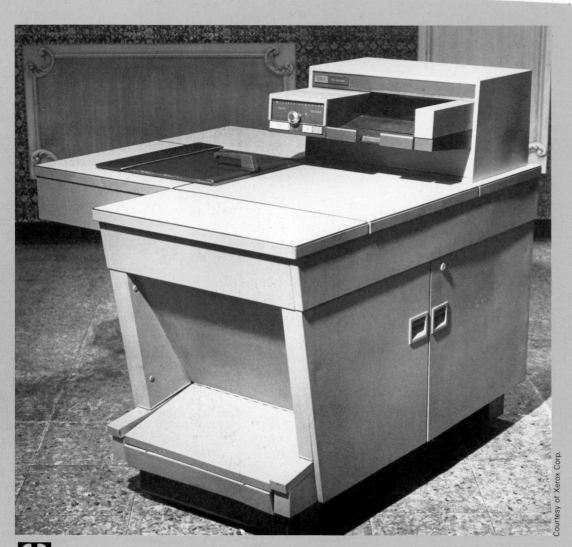

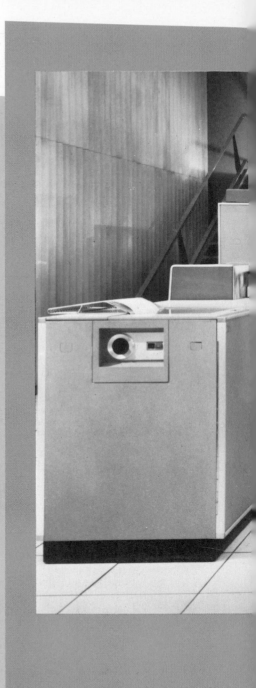

Courtesy of Xerox Corp.

This 1959 Xerox 914 copier qualifies as "Good Design." It was the first fully automatic office copying machine, operating on the electrostatic principles of xerography.

Courtesy of IBM

We have seen how, in some aspects of 1950s product design, wildly flashy style was all-important, how in other areas a bare-bones technological look was preferred, and how for some objects moderately flamboyant styling pepped up the drudgery for which they were intended. The designers of the new business machines of the decade—those invaluable copiers, computers, and recorders that helped huge corporations run more efficiently—took a middle road between these cardinal points. Their designs were simple, sober, and architectural, very much in keeping with the open-plan offices and glass-and-steel corporate headquarters in which the machines were installed.

Of course, the functional inner workings of these machines were anything but simple and in no way expressed by their outer appearance. To make a comparison, just as Mies van der Rohe could apply purely ornamental I-beams to the facade of the Seagram Building and still insist that its form *did* express its function, so too could Eliot Noyes—consultant director of design for IBM in the late 1950s—state that business machines "should be like a Mies house. They should have that much integrity and joy." If a computer's printed circuits were not visually coherent, they were simply concealed within its housing. Whether this was the joyful gesture of a designer with integrity is debatable. The fact of the matter is that it made the computer *look* a lot better. Now, as computers are readily being accepted in homes and business offices, designers are slowly beginning to rethink these structures—machines that will be a part of the daily routine—and to create more visually pleasing packages.

If 1950s cars, in all their gaudy splendor, embody a desire to escape America's puritan work ethic, the business machines of those years embody that ethic itself. Sharp-cornered, visually unified, and characterized by a regular repetition of uncluttered forms and stark shapes, these objects bespoke a business world that was cool, orderly, and efficient.

Under the leadership of Eliot Noyes, who in 1956 was IBM's Consultant Director of Design, computers like this one came to be distinguished by an architectural massing of its various parts. While not exactly bursting with peppy colors, these business machines did feature color-coded buttons and secondary colors to integrate irregular masses.

Package Deal

While the burst of consumerism during the fifties had its crass side, it is undeniable that the vast marketing effort made by manufacturers in those years led to the creation of beautifully designed selling "tools." During the 1930s—the years when industrial design became recognized as a profession in the United States—the industrial designer was viewed as a packager and, as such, more a business person than an artist. To those who believed that form must follow function, the streamlined designs of that decade and the early forties were only eye-catching, gimmicky gift-wrapping. It was not until after World War II that the form-follows-function industrial designers had their day. With the demand for a new, postwar "look" to consumer items, streamlining became more or less outmoded.

But the lessons of thirties industrial design were not lost on those designers called upon to package 1950s products. Indeed, many of them, like Raymond Loewy and Donald Deskey, had risen to prominence in the 1930s, their design philosophy unadulterated by Modernist principles. These designers, however, changed their styles in keeping with the times. And there were younger designers as well, who turned not to streamlined American design but to European Modernism for inspiration. Both younger and older designers created slick, unornamented, sculptural containers exuding the coolness and novelty that was deemed essential in the postwar years. (Hard sell was frowned upon in the fifties.)

Unlike the cars of that period, these containers—tubes, bottles, and boxes made of plastic, glass, or cardboard—were quite spare-looking. Their shapes—often hit upon only after extensive motivation research studies as to why a customer favors one sort of package over another—had a decidedly tactile quality that was meant to set a shopper's fingers tingling with desire. And when a package was made of then-new translucent or transparent plastic, the product (to quote a 1954 article in *Industrial Design*) had "an otherworldly effect," making it that much more appealing.

As in much 1950s graphic design, this packaging derived from contemporary fine art sources. Its sculptural forms, however, were chosen not for their original expressivity but for their memorability, which guaranteed quick, easy identification. Manufacturers liked the idea of instant identification. It meant that shoppers need not waste precious buying time reading labels; at most, they might be asked to recognize a logo, which required much less effort than reading. All a shopper had to do was see a package, recognize it, and—whammo—grab it off the shelf and buy it. The basic rules of package design certainly have not changed. And now, as we are leaving the past decades of revolutionary, all-new packages, we're seeing a return to more spare but stylized designs, similar to those of the fifties.

These striking packages consti-

Bristol-Myers packaged
Ban deodorant *(far left)* in a roll-
on dispenser made of polyeth-
ylene that made headlines in
design publications when it
was first launched in 1955.

What won't they think up
next? Today's Colgate
pump *(left)* is an eighties
equivalent of Ban's roll-on dispenser:
a clever, carefully thought-out packaging ploy that makes life easier for
the consumer—and makes money for
the manufacturer.

The jauntily syncopated
lettering on its box and its characteristic green hue made
Prell shampoo an easily identifiable product. Donald Deskey
designed this package in 1954,
but it would not look out of
place on a supermarket shelf
today.

tuted an endless cavalcade of hand-
some, clearcut forms, one more well-
executed and imaginative than the
next, and all simultaneously vying for
the consumer's attention. But these
packages *had* to be attention-getting.
For with suburban living proving to be
so desirable to a vast majority of Americans in the 1950s, the supermarket—
rather than the small neighborhood
grocery or drugstore—became the
new shopping arena. There, hundreds
of products were ranged on long
shelves along the aisles. Given the welter of visual information with which
each shelf bombarded the shopper, an
industrial designer needed to mobilize
all his forces in order to come up with a
package that would stand out from all
the rest.

Courtesy of Boeing Commercial Airplane Co.

Here Come the Planes

Walter Dorwin Teague Associates served as the designers for the Boeing 707 jet transport *(above left)*—a plane with a cruising speed of 550 miles an hour. It was first purchased by the U.S. Air Force. In summer 1955, it was offered to commercial airlines. Interestingly enough, fifties airplane interiors *(right)* do not look that significantly different from many of today's airplane interiors.

While the 1950s have occasionally been called the ''Jet Decade,'' in fact, America's first commercial jetliners did not start making flights until 1958. There is much about the jet plane, however, that makes it a fitting symbol of the 1950s, a decade shaped, in great part, by militarism. The first jets were fighter planes; it was World War II that brought about the technology of jet propulsion. And it was World War II that forged a generation of young pilots, thousands of whom had flown planes into combat. After their wartime experience, those men would not hesitate in the postwar years to become commercial pilots or, at least, to fly in civilian aircraft. Finally, it was victory in World War II that granted Americans, as citizens of the earth's most powerful nation, the right to go wherever they wanted in a world they could feel belonged to them—a right easily exercised by the jet.

The jet planes of the 1950s, then, were what the United States was as a nation: powerful, technologically advanced, and capable of going anywhere in the world. It was the industrial designer's job to convey all this to the public. The engineers who built the Boeing 707, the Douglas DC-8, and

Courtesy of Lockheed-California Co

the Convair 880 took care of the mechanics, which resulted in aircraft that varied in performance but basically resembled one another, with swept-back wings and clusters of jet pods. Indeed, these resemblances made the participation of an industrial designer all the more important. He was to style a jet for whichever commercial airline bought it, giving it a distinctive image through graphic, object, and interior design—an image that would fit in with an airline's overall corporate identity. That image would permit instant consumer identification and promote loyalty to an airline by investing it with an aura of power and modernity.

Today, while aircraft technology has made planes such as the Boeing 707 obsolete, airline identities remain what they were when they were created in the 1950s: cool, monolithic, masculine, and imbued with a sense of absolute, limitless freedom. Airline logos were abstract and memorable. Airplane interiors were orderly, clean-lined, spare, and wholly without reference to any interiors that passengers may have been in previously, as was only fitting for such unprecedented vehicles. Both the jet interiors and the paraphernalia of flying—everything from food trays to the crew's flight bags—featured a good deal of gleaming plastic. As for the exteriors, they were sleek and powerful-looking and painted with vivid ''jetlines'' that bespoke breathtaking speed. There was no attempt to ''humanize'' the jets, nor any attempt, as there had obviously been with cars, at playfulness or *joie de vivre*. Indeed, jet designers seemed to revel in the notion that, with these vehicles, Americans were exceeding earlier conceptions of human possibility and striving for new, unimagined heights. Having won World War II, Americans evidently needed neither consoling nostalgia nor a sense of humor. There was no place to go but up, up, and away into a future that was serious business. Americans were ready for that brave new world, and the jet planes of the late fifties were ready to whisk them around it in record time, enabling them to extend their dominance to every corner of the globe.

During the 1950s, many products embodied the Modernist "form follows function" outlook. Today, this outlook still informs much product design in America. Kitchen appliances, computers, power tools, jets—while all have undergone considerable technological development, their clean-lined, unornamented appearance has not changed all that much from the fifties, if only because their functional aspect is more important than their look.

More ephemeral and/or decorative products, ranging from ceramic trays to greeting cards to tableware, are starting to betray decidedly fifties influences in their design. In some instances, the flowing curves of, say, a metal salad bowl or porcelain teapot are quite reminiscent of the sober, elegant, high-style designs of the 1950s, whose spirit they imitate rather than transform. These, however, are exceptions, recalling as they do a side of fifties products that has been more or less ignored by today's designers in most other areas—that is, the emphasis on spare, functional, clean-lined

Ridiculously Practical

Courtesy of Evangeline Inc.

Asymmetrical quadrilaterals, these *Focal Points* ceramic trays recall a sign shape often seen on fifties roadside buildings. They were recently designed by James Johnson for Evangeline.

American automobile manufacturers know perfectly well that they will never be able to get away again with what they got away with in the fifties. And so the affection many Americans feel for these mythomobiles comes out in surprising ways; for example, in this chair *(left)*, a sort of merry-go-round version of a late 1950s Cadillac.

The sharp, skewed angles of the pieces in Kaneaki Fujimori's *Clouds* collection by Quantasia *(right)*, have a fifties tang to them.

design. Those who crave such pieces will be pleased to hear that many of the originals—particularly the dinnerware and serving pieces—are available in shops across the United States that specialize in fifties "antiques."

Other products evoke the more extravagantly futuristic designs that fall under the heading of fifties kitsch. Here the colors tend to be very much of today—lots of subtle pastels. The

forms, on the other hand—clunky, asymmetrical quadrilaterals and exaggerated "organic" curves—are pure 1950s pop (although, surprisingly enough, this feature is sometimes termed "art deco" by copywriters who are either misinformed or else feel that the term is more alluringly nostalgic than "fifties"). The message here, as with so many of today's fifties-inspired designs, is "fun." And al-

though these campy products can be functional, their humorous effect is the main point.

Fifties cars—what many view as the embodiment of America during that decade—are, obviously, no longer produced. But car customizers continue to work wonders on 1950s models that are still viable today, despite the fact that they were built to fall apart within one year's time. Some

favor faithfully restored fifties automobiles. Others take what were highly stylized creations to begin with and go their designers one better by adding exaggerations of their own. For those who cannot afford the real thing but still harbor a soft spot for those gas-guzzling behemoths, manufacturers are starting to come out with miniature replicas of the originals that are intended purely for display.

fashion loves nylons in colors that echo   your costume

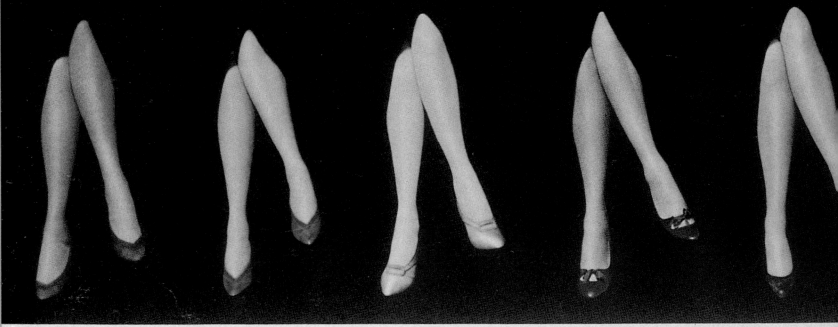

Fashion says: color-blend your costume. Fashion adds: *and don't forget your stockings.* Wear neutrals, yes. But have fun: this fall, have a rainbow in your stocking-box! A mist of blue for that blue slouch hat. A blush of red for a lacquer-red suit. Nylons in pale white, in loden green, brighter than ever . . . ever, too. Because tod more than just sheer. longer-wearing than an

CHEMSTRAN

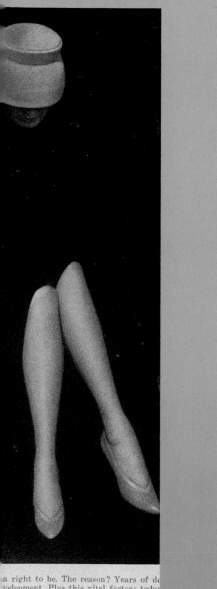

a right to be. The reason? Years of de
velopment. Plus this vital factor: today
a good share of nylon yarn is the produc
of the only integrated plant, the mos
modern research facilities, the most ex
citing name in nylon: Chemstrand.

2

Graphic Design

Space

With the dawn of the optimistic, everything-is-possible postwar era, images of freedom became a prime obsession among American designers with Modernist leanings. In fact, the spare, clean, look of Modern American graphic design derived from an aesthetic developed in Europe between the wars by the Bauhaus, the Russian constructivists, Dutch de Stijl designers, as well as by postwar Swiss graphic designers, whose purity paralleled that of earlier European styles. These movements all espoused a design that offered an alternative to the sentimental, richly ornamented kitsch beloved by the bourgeoisie since the mid-nineteenth century. Eschewing nostalgia, advocates of these movements devoted themselves to the present, emphasizing mass production, industrial technology, a keen appreciation of pure forms, and a utopian vision in which good design for all would lead to the collapse of the class system and to universal equality.

The fifties graphic designers who employed that Modernist idiom—many of them actually European émigrés fleeing fascism—did so in a somewhat less revolutionary spirit. Working in an American context, they were not so much breaking from bourgeois tradition as they were creating images that celebrated the power of a predominantly middle-class nation that, by 1950, was acknowledged as the strongest on earth. The placement of isolated or overlapping images in pristine expanses of empty space with a minimum of typography—that was typical of their designs—recalls similar characteristics of Modernist European graphics. For the European Modernists, all that space symbolized, in a sense, the tabula rasa of a Europe freed from the depredations of capitalism and due for radical social transfor-

While the B-52s often poke fun at early sixties rock in their music, the cover of their second album has definite fifties overtones: note the *Sculptura* chair (one of Woodard's big sellers) and the red infinity that serves as backdrop.

It's clear that nothing's going to get in *her* way.

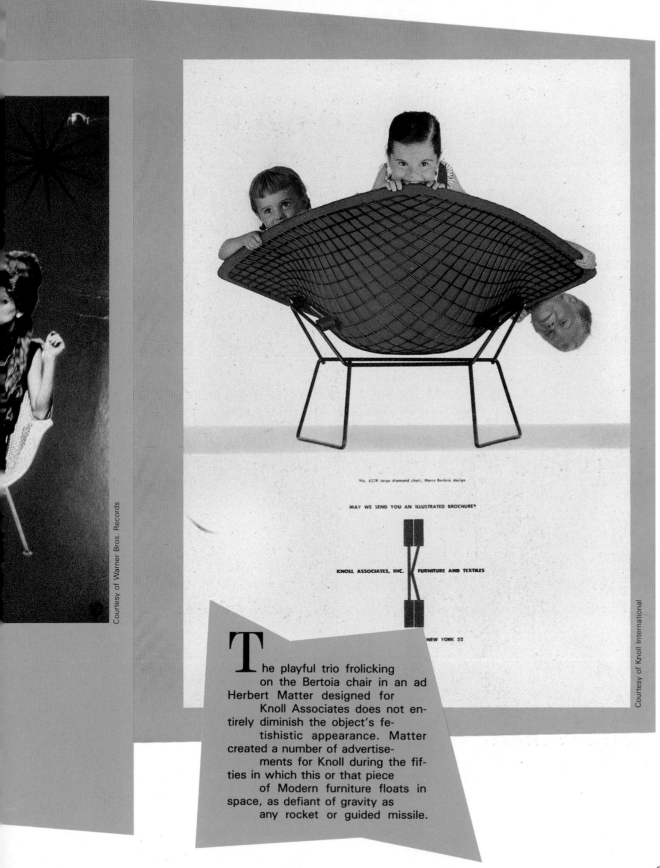

No. 422R large diamond chair, Harry Bertoia design

MAY WE SEND YOU AN ILLUSTRATED BROCHURE?

KNOLL ASSOCIATES, INC. FURNITURE AND TEXTILES

NEW YORK 22

The playful trio frolicking on the Bertoia chair in an ad Herbert Matter designed for Knoll Associates does not entirely diminish the object's fetishistic appearance. Matter created a number of advertisements for Knoll during the fifties in which this or that piece of Modern furniture floats in space, as defiant of gravity as any rocket or guided missile.

mation. In American graphics, on the other hand, space constituted a new expression of the capitalistic spirit of manifest destiny. In advertisements and magazines of the 1950s, Americans were offered the very image of their triumphantly bourgeois nation's future: a vast tract, not of land, but of time, that beckoned with boundless possibilities for technological growth.

It should be noted that not all 1950s graphics were characterized by empty space and uniform typefaces sparingly deployed across the page. In fact, this particular style was evident not so much in ads as in the decade's magazine covers and layouts—especially in those of fashion magazines, where blank space offered an ideal backdrop for the crisp silhouettes of fifties women's clothing. Advertisements, on the other hand, came, as we shall see, in a multiplicity of styles. However, when the space "look" *was* employed, it usually served to sell a sophisticated consumer a high-end item—a bottle of costly perfume, say, or a designer chair.

In both ads and editorials, that spacious look featured a minimal use of type. It was as if words were too mundane, too earthbound, too finite to do justice to the infinity of empty space. Capital letters were often omitted, as if even they would upset the overall purity. In its (usually) white void, the image—whether perfume bottle or chair—soared, full of the dynamic vitality with which fifties America pulsated. There, with all superfluous ornamentation swept away and colors limited for the most part to primaries and black, the product was endowed with maximum legibility. Cleansed and held aloft from the murky crosscurrents of daily life, it conveyed the brisk, up-to-the-minute image fifties manufacturers were eager to project. What's more, that image fixed the product in the buyer's mind. Indeed, yanked from its context in reality and set against empty space, the commodity took on a glamorous, almost sacred quality. It became fascinating in and of itself, quite apart from its function—a curious paradox, if we recall that functionality was a concern of America's Modernist designers.

One catches a whiff of Russian constructivism in the IBM logo *(left),* developed in the 1950s and still in use today. The revolutionary spirit which imbued the inspirations for this logo might horrify IBM. The *look* of revolution, on the other hand, proved thoroughly applicable to its aims.

Abstractions

"Fine Art" influences on fifties graphic design *(rig*h seem most appropriate when it is fine art (in this case, Tchaikovsky symphony) that the design is advertising.

Given the public's dislike of abstract art, the preponderance of abstract forms and patterns in 1950s graphic design derived from such art might appear somewhat surprising. After all, a visual idiom that shattered the supposedly falsifying constraints of realism—the preferred style of the bourgeoisie—seems an unlikely means of aiding a most realistic and bourgeois pursuit, that is, making money.

Yet by the 1940s some of America's more enlightened businessmen were coming to recognize the power of the abstract image. That image was simple, direct, contemporary-looking, and—perhaps most important—it stuck in people's minds. Sophisticated and current, the abstract image also contained a certain emotional power. In a 1957 issue of *Art Direction,* one writer went so far as to key major twentieth-century artists according to the emotional connotations of their paintings, with the obvious aim of suggesting whose imagery would serve as an appropriate model for the advertising of this or that product. Paul Klee's imagery, for example, supposedly bespoke frivolity and childish impulsiveness, while Wassily Kandinsky's symbolized feelings run amok.

The public may have ignored the art magazines where the work of these artists was reproduced. They may have avoided the museums where their abstract paintings were shown. But the graphic designs featuring similarly abstract imagery that confronted them in newspapers, magazines, and on television, as well as on a vast amount of printed matter ranging from corporate annual reports to restaurant menus, was seen as an expression not of idiosyncratic, intellectual "artists" but of the Zeitgeist. They embodied the very spirit of the fifites. As such, they met with a favorable response.

Perhaps the most communicative abstract imagery that figured in the graphic design of the 1950s was to be found in the corporate logos that were developed during the period. Prior to the 1950s, most corporate identities tended to be rather cumbersome affairs. The acceptance of Modernism by powerful corporations wishing to

Tchaikovsky

Symphony No. 5 IN E MINOR, OP. 64

Antal Dorati CONDUCTING THE

Minneapolis Symphony Orchestra

LONG PLAYING
MERCURY
CLASSICS

Courtesy of Polygram Records, Inc.

impress the public with their orderliness, newness, and efficiency changed that. Numerous corporations updated their images, not only by establishing themselves in new glass-and-steel headquarters but also by identifying themselves with new logos that appeared on everything from their stationery to their nationwide magazine and television advertisements. Indeed, these stark, unornamented and usually symmetrical forms had the same sleek, impersonal air as those glass-and-steel corporate headquarters. Like them, they bespoke tremendous power and advanced technology. Even when composed of no more than a few letters, a logo could take on an impressively monumental, if somewhat dehumanized, appearance.

Surely this could not have been what, say, Kandinsky had in mind when he conceived of abstract art as a means of expressing the most profound urges of the human spirit. The decade's graphic designers, in fact, were well aware of the contradictions that arose in applying fine art ideals to marketing methods. The debate as to whether contemporary art and graphic design were enriching big business or being co-opted by it continued throughout the fifties. Nowhere was this conflict more evident than in the way abstract art, avant-garde though it was, was thoroughly assimilated by the corporate mentality, which used it for its own ends. Even the abstract expressionism of the late forties and fifties provided grist for the corporate mill, for example, with stark, Franz Kline-esque brushstrokes framing the photo of a new Plymouth in a magazine ad.

The co-optation versus enrichment debate was never resolved. Today, in looking at these graphic abstractions, one has to admit to a sense of pleasure that such imaginative and persuasive images were *not* merely relegated to museums. They actually *did* enrich the texture of daily life. Yet one is also dismayed by what this use of abstract art by commerce implied: that is, that every work of art, no matter how exalted or unique the inspiration behind it, could easily be turned into a selling tool.

Order and Disorder

Graphic designer Alvin Lustig created images of both order and disorder for two New Directions paperbacks. While both books are still in print, their covers are not like any being designed right now. Those evocative juxtapositions are gentler, sadder than today's images.

Three Tragedies by Lorca

Lorca

3 tragedies

Courtesy of New Directions

NDP52

CAMINO REAL
TENNESSEE *Williams*
NEW DIRECTIONS

Courtesy of New Directions

NDP301

ALMOST

big

Courtesy of Riviera Productions Ltd.

This eighties album cover, with its image of frayed edges and disparate typefaces in wildly contrasting scales, could easily be taken for a fifties original.

many 1950s graphics were an expression of the same outlook that favored abstract imagery. Here, however, the inspiration was provided, for the most part, by the severe, rectilinear compositions of one artist—Piet Mondrian. The collagiste aesthetic, on the other hand, had its roots in cubism, as well as the more anarchic style of the dadaists. Sometimes the casualness of the collage ''look'' would creep into the compartmentalized ''look,'' so that the outlines of those neat boxes would become wavy and inexact. The boxes themselves were deployed asymmetrically across the page: perky, yes, but also rigid. Both styles were used to sell everything from literature to jewelry to white bread to shares of stock.

Both these trends—collage and compartmentalization—provide further evidence of the way in which graphic designers appropriated fine art motifs. Indeed, craftspeople and designers of wallpaper and fabrics borrowed such motifs, too. Although their output is often labeled applied, or decorative, art, it in fact often rivaled the models on which it was based. It might be argued that designers cheapened cubism, dadaism, and Mondrian's minimalist aesthetic by creating graphics whose primary purpose was to sell something. But the infiltration of imagery associated with these styles into commercial art—an infiltration that had begun in the 1940s and reached its peak in the following decade—lent a vibrant quality to advertisments and magazines that made them more than mere commodities. The leading lights of the various European art and design movements that so influenced 1950s American graphic design had dreamed of integrating quality design into daily life. Such an integration, they believed, would improve life itself—a rather unrealistic hope, perhaps. But if the Mondrian-inspired boxes and their diametric opposites, the collages of fifties graphics, did not alter daily life, they certainly lent it a sense of beauty and stylishness that took the edge off capitalist competitiveness and the dry, hard facts of a market economy, and reached the masses in a way that fine art itself could not.

Much American graphic design of the fifties betrays not only the contradictions between big business and art but also those besetting the nation itself. The United States was relaxing and enjoying the pleasures of economic prosperity—and adhering to a rigid conformism. Graphics of the decade suggested these contradictions in the simultaneous appearance of some designs in which sharply demarcated compartments and boxes figured prominently, and others in which images and type were arranged in a random, collagelike fashion that emphasized incongruous objects and typefaces and contrasting textures.

The compartments that figure in so

Art by Jim Heimann

Jim Heimann serves up an *Atomic TV Dinner* in this recent illustration.

Homey Clutter

Through a process of rapid evolution, the collagiste aesthetic apparent in some 1950s graphics gave rise to one of homey clutter. Homey clutter-type advertisments boasted images arranged asymmetrically, in seemingly random fashion. Here, however, no fine art influence tempered the cheerful but clearly hard-sell aspect of the ad. A hodgepodge of garishly colored photos or realistic, carefully rendered, and straightforwardly presented illustrations of products—foods, especially canned foods; people; and domestic vignettes—all offered a vision of Amer-

ican clean living in which family "togetherness," idealized romance, and economic prosperity blended. Type in such ads was plentiful, empty space nearly nonexistent.

While many of the decade's art directors felt that ads should flatter the public's sense of style, the creators of such homey-looking graphics were aiming for Middle America all the way—a Middle America that did not necessarily give a hoot about modern art. As such, their exuberant but unsophisticated designs might be construed as a more accurate mirror of

American taste. (It was these ads, incidentally, and *not* the decade's more refined graphics, that provided the pop artists of the sixties with their inspiration.) It is strange, though, to leaf through a magazine from the decade and come across plain and earthy, sometimes totally banal ads, without so much as a smattering of European influence, side by side with superbly composed, streamlined, cosmopolitan graphic compositions. Indeed, the sheer variety of ads within one issue of a 1950s magazine provides excellent proof of the diversity of the fifties style.

During the fifties, magazines ranging from *Good Housekeeping* to *House Beautiful* to *Life* ran ads like these two. Unlike much graphic design of those years, these bear no trace of aesthetic pretension. The main idea is abundance, messy rather than pristine. A smell of canned tomato soup seems to rise off them.

The colors of such ads often had a slightly stale look. And yet they were evidently what the marketing people felt middle-of-the-road consumers would understand and salivate over.

OUP for a
ry special supper!

tomato soup   1 can mushroom soup   RITZ CRACKERS

your fussiest aunt will enthuse over this *new* "Tomato Surprise"! Combine the two soups and, if condensed, add equal amount of Fill a sautéed mushroom cap with whipped cream and float on Serve with her favorite RITZ CRACKERS. They're a teasing, tangy ... the very *crispest* of all crackers! They pay respect to *any* guest re just the most *delicious* form of flattery! For everyone who knows d food appreciates RITZ CRACKERS — loves the way they give the lest meal that "very special" flavor!

"NOTHING TASTES AS GOOD AS RITZ—BUT RITZ!"

the best when it's baked by Nabisco
NAtional
BIScuit
COmpany

RITZ CRACKERS

Ideal summer lunch...for kids at home...for dad at work!

soup 'n sandwiches

Good 'n quick! Good 'n delicious! Good 'n nourishing!

Campbell's Tomato Soup with whipped cream, cream-cheese and nut-bread sandwich

Make soup your one hot dish with cool summer meals!

Cold sandwich? Add a bowl of soup! That's such a welcome meal—because soup supplies the one hot dish often neglected in summer.

There are so many different Campbell's Soups brimming with the natural goodness

your family needs to go on and grow on. And every one makes a sandwich taste better!

Campbell's Soups are such a good value in pleasure, thrift and nutrition. How's your summer supply?

Have you had your soup today?

Campbell's
CONDENSED
SOUP

SOUP SANDWICH CENTER
Look for this sign at your grocer's

Fifties graphic designers were well aware of the trends in contemporary European painting of their day and were quick to borrow its imagery (if not its content) for advertisements. Styles as diverse as Bauhaus Modernism and dadaism were borrowed. Another European style—surrealism—proved equally inspiring. In their paintings, surrealist artists like Salvador Dali, Yves Tanguy, and René Magritte, as well as the proto-surrealist Giorgio de Chirico, sought to evoke the unfathomable, mysterious quality of inanimate objects by depicting them in idealized landscapes or cityscapes. American graphic designers of the 1950s were not so much suggesting an object's poetic dimension as emphasizing its desirability by placing it in the dreamlike settings beloved of surrealists.

Much advertising of the 1950s used this surrealist technique and qualified as surrealist art (or, in the case of television commercials, film) in and of itself. Products appeared amid scenery that was at once disturbingly unfamiliar and strangely alluring. Americans did not mistake these weird tableaux for scenes from the Good Life—but then, that was not what advertisers had in mind. Rather, the Madison Avenue movers saw the fine art origins of these "arty" ads as flattering the sensibilities of a public sure to buy a tasteful product that would bring a dreamy and, more to the point, highbrow quality to its possessor's life.

In some advertisements, the surrealistic imagery assumes a science fiction tone. Here, technological utopias stretch off into a distance that is the visible symbol of the intangible, invisible, and distant future. They are bathed in the same cold sunlight that illuminates de Chirico's metaphysical piazzas—a sunlight whose clarity does little to reveal the true meaning of the objects upon which it falls. While advertisers intended these images to convey a positive sense of scientific progress, the effect, more often than not, is a bit alienating. Those clean, orderly utopias, impressive and idealized though they are, ultimately seem uninhabitable.

Dreams that Money Can Buy

Faceless, mannequinlike figures out of de Chirico via fifties graphics grace this eighties album jacket. It is strange that, while the Italian master's paintings often convey a sense of menace and anguish, the humanoids who in part contributed to that feeling were used in 1950s graphics—and in this contemporary, fifties-derived image—to convey a sense of a bracingly cold but thrilling future: It is as if, by the 1950s, it was no longer all right to be completely human, as if it were the wave of the future to become an automaton.

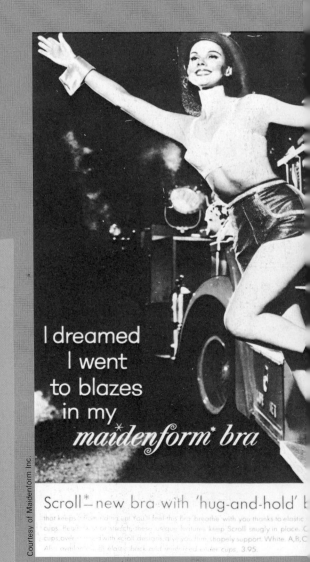

The strange disjunction of scales in this fifties ad, as well as the woman's having appeared inexplicaby in the sky, recall surrealist painting's odd juxtapositions.

John Rawlings. Courtesy of the Edward C. Blum Design Laboratory, The Fashion Institute of Technology

One would not expect psychoanalysis to lend itself to selling women's undergarments; yet in the 1950s it was a selling point. Recent ads—particularly some for perfumes—have a similarly dream-like yet slicker quality.

Surrealistic imagery in fifties graphics was also used to convey a feeling of dark sexuality. Ads presented dimly lit and/or veiled scenes full of tantalizing mystery. Still unliberated by the sexual revolution that was a decade off, repressed fifties Americans must have seen these designs as expressions of their own unacknowledged and undefined yearnings. These, advertisers reasoned, could be easily sublimated with the purchase of whatever commodity that enigmatic ad touted.

Finally, there were similarly dark, surrealistic ads that were not so much sexual as hallucinatory. Disembodied gloved hands appearing from out of nowhere; a half-opened door in a black void; melting, Daliesque watches—these, too, captured people's attention thanks to their bizarre quality, even though what they were advertising was no more bizarre than a new typewriter or life insurance policy. Again, the ad's effectiveness resided in the "artiness" of its imagery; its morbid, disconcerting quality was secondary. The main message had to do with the product's classiness—a classiness it would confer on its owner.

Smiley

American advertisers of the 1950s left no emotion untapped in their tireless efforts to attract the consumer's notice. Perhaps the most entertaining—and most insidious—technique used was the cartoon. Billboards, television commercials, and advertisements teemed with goofy, freely drawn characters whose beaming faces and endearingly klutzy air were meant to so warm the heart that a consumer could not resist shelling out cash for whatever product this personage happened to be hawking. Unlike the animated characters emanating from the Disney studio, these cartoons bore scant resemblance to real people. Indeed, they might be no more than sticks of margarine with hopeful eyes and silly grins.

Advertisers felt that the cartoon characters enlivening their ads would fix their products more firmly in people's minds. What's more, they would provide people with free, if fleeting entertainment, so as to make them feel obscurely in the advertiser's debt the next time they went out shopping. But these memorable and imaginatively conceived figures served another purpose, too: that is, to give the impression that the manufacturer was a friendly fellow, almost childlike, and in no way likely to try selling you a deficient bill of goods. The consumer could tolerate those figures, amid the nearly intolerable ad bombardment, just because they were so cute. Kids, even more susceptible to the appeal of imaginary beings than their parents, would find them irresistible and clamor for the product with which they were identified.

Cartoon characters in 1950s graphics numbered in the thousands, with one more friendly looking than the next. In retrospect, this friendliness now seems very mechanical and somewhat insincere. The manufacturers these cartoon characters advertised were friendly only insofar as they wanted to make a sale. Beyond that, it was strictly a question of the bottom line, that is, nothing to smile about. Yes, one laughing beaker or companionable tiger was amusing. A few might constitute a lovable menagerie, a pleasant change from the more realistic photographs and illustrations that filled many other advertisements. But after awhile the good cheer seemed unnatural. The happy eyes looked glazed, the smiles creepily permanent. And, their laughable and clumsily rendered anatomies notwithstanding, the cartoons become grinning robots, programmed to ingratiate themselves to one and all.

Yet it is this programmed good cheer—along with the invariably cockeyed typography that heightened it—that proves so fascinating. During the 1950s, America's designers created a multitude of easily read symbols wholly devoid of content. The smiling cartoon figure symbolized Friendliness—period. The ballerina, her figure repeated ad infinitum across a roll of wallpaper, symbolized Fine Art—period. The molecule symbolized Benevolent Technology. All were to be accepted at face value. *Was* big business all that amiable? *Did* the arts play a meaningful role in American life? And what about those technological advances? That deeply most people chose not to delve. Instead, sign was mistaken for reality. Complex reality—the *real*, possibly unnerving and certainly contradictory reality—went conveniently ignored. Simple signs were reality enough, perhaps all the reality anybody could take in the dawning nuclear age. Seen in this light, those wacky cartoon faces become eerie, masklike.

© Billboard Art 1984 Landau/Henderson

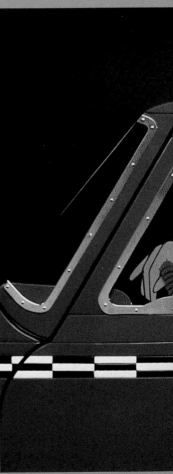

The smiling skinhead in Dan Dailey's 1982 metal-and-glass *Fern-O (right)* could have figured in the graphics preceding the broadcast of a 1950s sitcom—maybe one in which Ralph Cramden loses a lot of weight, shaves his head, and decides to drive a taxi instead of a bus. The background music would have been jazzy but not too hot, to get the home audience in the mood for a good time—but first, a word from our sponsor.

If the parading sucking candies in this fifties ad *(far right)* had faces, they would surely be smiling ones.

L ittle Lulu *(left)* pointing to a box of tissues on this 1950s billboard may strike you as endearing. She is one of many examples of cartoon influence in fifties graphic design.

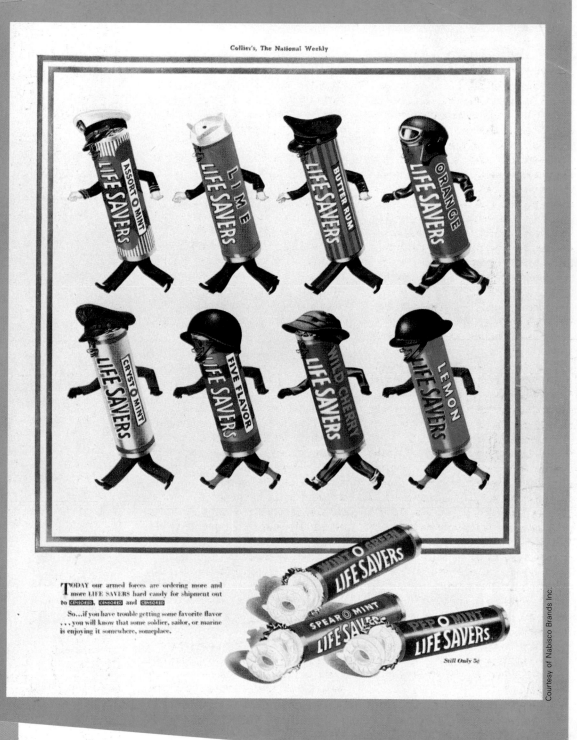

Courtesy of Kurland Summers Gallery

Courtesy of Nabisco Brands Inc.

Two characteristics of fifties graphics—the ''arty'' look recalling this or that contemporary art style and the freely drawn cartoon figures—were combined in the frequent use of freehand, unfinished-looking illustrations and lettering. This imagery was derived from the cubist art of Pablo Picasso and Juan Gris, as well as from the lyrical compositions of Paul Klee, Joan Miró, Henri Matisse, and Stuart Davis—painters who, prior to the rise of the abstract expressionists of the New York School, constituted the latest word in modernity, with a touch of European (in Davis's case, European-style) ''class.''

In some instances, the advertisements that were based on the work of these artists, with their skewed, scratchily incised lines and quirky figures, have a carefree, humorous air. In others, the intentionally rough-edged lettering and asymmetrical, floating blocks of solid color create a gripping, dramatic mood. In both its manifestations, such imagery spelled out one word: ''modern.''

It is curious that so many of the decade's graphics have a hand-drawn

Free-Hand

The skewed, cut-out letters and shapes of this 1950s album cover *(far left)* provide a visual echo of the jazz contained therein.

In his design for a poster advertising the 1985 revival of an O'Neill drama *(left)*, Daniel Geisler recalls "razor blade technique" featured in some fifties graphics.

One Andrew Warhol designed this book jacket *(right)* for the New Directions hardcover edition of three Firbank novels. Today, when illustrators give figures this kind of freely drawn look, they exaggerate the freeness wildly to suggest eighties near-hysteria.

Saul Bass, one of the fifties' most noted graphic designers, created a series of striking advertisements for films, including *Anatomy of a Murder (far right)*.

look—even when they were advertising something as technologically unprecedented as television. The crooked lines, uneven edges, blotchy colors, and effortless quality of both illustrations and lettering, as well as the almost sloppy appearance of the layouts, suggested the individual with his warm-though-fallible hands and fecund creativity; cold, implacable machines or sterile, anonymous corporations were not even hinted at.

Seen in this light, the imagery speaks of yet another paradox within the fifties style: on the one hand, its references to contemporary painting stood for modernity; on the other hand, its artlessness told of simple humanity prevailing in the face (or facelessness) of the modern world with its corporate hierarchies, automation, and too-rapid scientific progress. Of course, these ads were paid for by the very organizations whose omnipotence their somewhat disorganized imagery seemed to deny, and they were mechanically reproduced in the hundreds of thousands. But neither fact took away from the imagery's appearance of having been drawn freehand by an individual, in a mood far more whimsical than that which predominated in ultraserious big business.

This was exactly how big businesses wanted it. They did not care to present themselves as exploiters hellbent on profit. Rather, this was just one more example of how they were shown to be the consumer's friend.

During the fifties, many advertisers made a point, in their hand-drawn imagery, of seeming to be playful and mild-mannered. But twice as many advertisers sought to overwhelm the consumer by presenting their products in ads that featured monolithic images. Posters, magazine and newspaper ads, and especially billboards boasted images of commodities photographed and presented in such a way that they appeared at once as works of art (not just something you picked up off the shelf and paid for) and magical objects

advertisements in which contextless images were presented unencumbered by words. With television, Americans became hooked on the image. Words seemed too specific. What's more, one had to read them, and that took time. The image, on the other hand, instantly communicated its primary message.

That people perceived the image's message subliminally made it all the more potent. Indeed, one of World War II's many "benefits" was the importation of Freudian psychology to

kind of identity was especially important in the fifties when, because brand differences were minor, loyalty to a particular product had to be cultivated through image. Simple, memorable, and overwhelming, the image engraved itself in the consumer's mind.

The Big Image prevailed in editorials as well as in advertisements. In highly successful large-format illustrated magazines such as *Life* and *Look,* photographs took precedence over words (*Life* went so far as to develop a typeface ideally suited to photographs and

The Photographic Image

guaranteed to fulfill one's every desire.

Most of these images encouraged the consumer to accept the modern, technological world and, in the increased leisure time and shorter work hours it provided, to revel in the sensual pleasures that world afforded. It was technology, after all, that made these images possible—the technologies of photography and of offset lithography, the two together conspiring to make the product seem realer than real. And it was the technology of mass production that made the commodities advertised available in such endless quantities.

It was not only the triumph of technology that these ads celebrated; it was the triumph of the image. Although surrealist painting and photography were influential, it was television that convinced art directors to offer

America, where its interpretations of the dreaming mind's image-repertoire were seized on by market researchers, ad people, art directors, and commercial photographers. All were willing to persuade consumers to buy a product by enumerating its advantages (in minimal copyblocks set in sleek, unobtrusive typefaces) and by psychologically manipulating consumers with the images that comprised the language of their unconscious.

The seductive Big Image of 1950s ads, whether presented in magazines and newspapers or blown up to gargantuan proportions on the billboards lining the newly paved highways, tempted the consumer with its promise to satisfy the most infantile desires; it also—along with its more abstract cohort, the logo—gave a product an instantly recognizable identity. That

guaranteed not to draw attention away from them to the purely secondary text). Fashion magazines emphasized the Big Image as well, to create a vivid aura of sophisticated worldliness more quickly and convincingly than words.

Yes, the picture was worth a thousand words. But the picture, especially the photographic Big Image, could also conquer a thousand *worlds*. Anything—anything in the world—could be photographed and, thus appropriated, captured between the covers of a magazine. Indeed, it is no wonder that the photographic image loomed so large in graphic design during a decade when America felt as if it *could* have whatever it wanted. That image bespoke not only products that overwhelmed consumers but also a country capable of appropriating the planet.

INDULGE

Knoll tantalized potential consumers with this fasc[in]ing, unknown object veiled in a plain brown wrapper *(right* object whose mystery was only emphasized by the that it was presented as a photograph of something rather than a drawing of something imagined. (A follow-u[p] showed what was underneath: a smartly dressed fas[hion] model perched on Eero Saarinen's pedestal chair. campaigns for recent films like *Ghostbusters* and *Turk 18[2]* starting off with posters featuring an unexplained log[o or] phrase, are latter-day attempts at fifties-style tantalization

Gigantic images of food or beverages like the one on this fifties billboard *(left)* promised all the instant gratification you could handle. In time, many Americans came to see billboards as landscape spoilers. What they ignored was the surrealistic dimension these creatures brought to our country's highways.

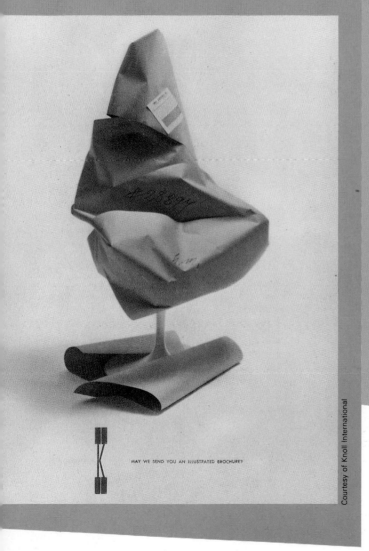

MAY WE SEND YOU AN ILLUSTRATED BROCHURE?

N° 5

CHANEL

PERFUME

Through the simple yet dramatic composition of this ad for Chanel perfume, the image of the product alone conveys the selling message.

In many ways, advertising art of the fifties was quite different from that of today: both the cluttered, unsophisticated and the artistic 1950s designs are things of the past. But the use of photographic images of human beings in situations that immediately involve viewers—an approach that was honed to perfection in the fifties—still prevails.

In graphics that stressed the human factor, the picture, art directors hoped, *was* worth a thousand words. Leading photographers of the day provided

peddling a product too shrilly was an insult to the public. The "fast sell" was preferable—fast and cool. Type—most frequently Century Schoolbook, touted in a 1956 issue of *Art Direction* as the decade's most popular advertising typeface—tended to be black on a white background, or vice versa. The overall impression the typography gave was one of calmness. After the entertaining image, it gave a sense of getting down to business and telling the public what the product was *really* like, evenly, persuasively, with no competi-

Fifties ads often made wry reference to the war between the sexes. In this billboard advertisement for Pepsi-Cola *(above),* a worldly woman seems to be gently chiding her companion for his taciturn behavior. The dry tone is further emphasized with that casual command to "Be Sociable," in a feminine script that has something high-society about it.

The human element is still a key factor in ads like this one for Coca-Cola *(right).* Here, however, the models are posed in a more relaxed manner than they would have been in the fifties. Perhaps thirty years hence we will discern just how stylized their "naturalism" is.

The Human Factor

crisp, hard-edged, uncluttered images of people in glamorous, intriguing, funny, or sexually suggestive situations. Without saying anything specific about the product, these images captured one's attention. They stuck in the mind. What copy the ad included—perhaps a phrase wittily punning on the picture, followed by a block of smaller type giving specific information about the product—might then be read, though it was always the photo that drew attention, not the words.

The look of these ads tended to be cool and clean—no collage effects, no abstract designs, no scratchily incised, cockeyed lettering or intentionally imprecise layouts. More to the point, there was no attempt at hard sell. Advertising wisdom of the time held that

tive claims or false hype: the graphic equivalent of the emotionally neutral man in the gray flannel suit (a uniform, incidentally, which in the 1950s was first associated with Madison Avenue admen).

Colorful or monochromatic photographs of people, however, were the main attraction in these ads. No doubt the widespread use of these graphics was a response to the public's taste for picture magazines like *Look* and *Life,* both of which were packed with "human interest" stories in which living was presented as an action-filled and eminently "illustratable" process. Even more significant, though, was the influence of television and its ability, noted by McLuhan, to involve viewers instantly in the lives of whichever people, real or fictitious, happened to

Here the war between the sexes veers into coyness, as the woman wraps the man around her little finger *(right)*.

with **RED TAPE** in MAX Factor's Color-fast **lipstick**

new ruby red winding through the whole fashion scene

the only non-smear type lipstick with stay-on lustre

appear on the tube. Like characters in the decade's television sitcoms, the men, women, and children in 1950s ads often had a relaxed, natural, every-day air about them (the chic, highly stylized fashion ads, of course, were exceptions) with which people easily identified. Indeed, many photographs depicted likable-looking people in ab-surd situations to which they appeared to respond with resignation and a win-ning wryness. These elicited sympathy from the public, who could readily imagine themselves in such hilariously bewildering circumstances. The ads, of course, flatteringly implied that they, too, would rise above such circum-stances, sense of humor intact.

The "human factor" approach re-sulted in some of the fifties' most clever advertisements. In them, dry wit prevailed. The art directors, copywrit-ers, and photographers of such ads seemed to be saying that they found advertisements as irritating and unnec-essary as many consumers did—and still do. Therefore, rather than shout their sales pitch, they undercut it, im-plying that people, and not products, were what's most important to them. This, of course, was just a more subtle sales pitch. But throughout the 1950s this ironic, blasé, hey-let's-face-it-we're-all-in-this-together tone did not fail to win a customer's sympathy and business.

The influence of 1950s graphic design on today's graphics is most evident in current record album jackets, mainly those aimed at the young market for New Wave music. With few exceptions, these eighties designs, with their bright, warm colors and jumble of typefaces, would never be mistaken for fifties originals. They are too exaggerated, too campy. As such, they reflect the same contemporary sensibility that favors recycled 1950s teen fashions—a sensibility that both ridicules and enjoys the ridiculousness of naively optimistic, consumer-crazed postwar America. This same America has now spawned a ''cool,'' supposedly sophisticated nihilism among young people who view their surroundings with condescension; and thanks to a less ''cool'' anxiety over the present world political struggle, fifties America elicits all sorts of nostalgic yearnings.

These album graphics often have a manic quality that is much more in keeping with New Wave music than with the actual fifties style. Often they

High-Tack

Beauty on the Beach: Dressed in her prim, no-nonsense, one-piece fifties bathing suit, this playful siren could have stepped out of a *Mademoiselle* fashion plate, circa 1957. However, the lines of the background (radiation?) definitely place this announcement card for one of New York City's most popular clubs right where it belongs: smack in the middle of the 1980s.

Art by Susan Faiola

Illustrator Susan Faiola's goofy recycling of fifties motifs takes on an eighties knowingness thanks to the picture's candy-sweet colors, the kind graphic designers of the 1950s might have found a bit too extreme.

incorporate motifs from 1950s furniture and textile designs and roadside architectural signs. Many characteristically fifties graphic styles—the collagiste approach, say, or the freehand look—are not alluded to at all. Nevertheless, today's graphic designers do succeed in summoning up the 1950s with a handful of images that are most quickly associated with that time. While many 1950s graphic designers were trying to both upgrade and flatter the public's sense of style with self-consciously artistic designs, today's fifties-ish graphics are meant to have a comically "tacky" quality.

The fifties influence appears in some of today's magazine layouts, too. More empty space is showing up on the page, as are cockeyed lettering, perky-looking little dart and boomerang shapes, and asymmetrical triangles. These contemporary graphics are much less raucous than those enlivening record albums, and their intent is less satirical, more good-natured. Indeed, it is not always easy to determine exactly why fifties references have been used at all, aside from their providing yet another new, "fun" look for the readership. As for the luxuriously large formats that characterized many 1950s magazines, those belong—with a few exceptions—to a decade far more prosperous and wasteful than ours.

Art by Mike Fink

for unruly hair

O D E L L

Those men who were boys in the fifties may remember Odell, the viscous, milky hair tonic used to slick down unruly locks. In Mike Fink's recent graphic design *(left)*, however, the Odell has apparently been used to slick the guy's hair up into a reasonable ducktail. The cockeyed letters—while they have nothing in common with the plain orange, black, and white label on the Odell bottle—are certifiably fifties.

This coffee shop from another planet *(right)* swirls into our solar system in another update of fifties graphic design format. The cup and saucer seem to have dropped out of the wild blue yonder, while the sun-stars revolve around the 24-hour-a-day coffee shop where a handful of change scattered on the counter still buys a cup of coffee as it did in the fifties. The tilted letters and seemingly random design are derivative of that decade, but don't fail to notice the eighties graffiti motif in the upper right corner.

Art by Mike Fink

3
Craft Objects

Plain and Simple

During the 1950s, American craftspeople—potters, weavers, metal and wood workers, enamelists, and so on—felt embattled on many fronts. On the one hand, the country's most forward-looking architects and designers were singing the praises of functionality, machine technology, and mass production, and they were deriding decoration. On the other hand, the New York School artists were seizing the spotlight with their abstract expressionist canvases that were immediately recognized as high art, statements supposedly delivered up from the depths of the artist's soul, as opposed to craft objects, which were "merely" decorative. As for the critics, most of them seemed to feel that handicrafts, unlike the buildings of Mies van der Rohe and Frank Lloyd Wright or the paintings of Jackson Pollock and Willem de Kooning, gave them little to sink their teeth into. Consequently, the kind of heated polemics that went on around, and provided such excellent publicity for, artists and architects were virtually unknown in the world of 1950s American crafts.

Given all this, it is no wonder that so few museums and collectors paid much attention to American craft objects in the fifties. If designers used them at all, it was mainly as sparingly deployed accessories in their hard-edged Modern interiors. As for the average consumers, they were too busy gobbling up mass-produced items for their homes and embracing whatever new fad came along, whether it was in clothes, in automobiles, or in decor.

It appears, then, that in many ways crafts, and the mystique of the handmade object, were out of step with the times. What support crafts did receive came from a small group of forward-thinking designers, small liberal arts colleges and design schools, and a handful of gallery owners and museums. The craftspeople, however, did not let this faze them. Indeed, they seemed to draw strength and a sense of identity from their position. As potter Marguerite Wildenhain noted in 1959, in her book *Pottery: Form and Expression*, the truly dedicated craftsperson chooses "not money, nor success, nor power, nor the machine, but man, the very genuine essence of man." The mission of the American craftsperson in the 1950s, according to Wildenhain, was far more important than most people realized. "We know that there are many men and women . . . deeply disturbed by the current materialistic trend. . . . It is essential to give them affirmation and hope, to coordinate all their efforts into a more conscious group of honest workers towards an aim that has human dignity and personal integrity."

Among craftspeople, this belief in the very human values that fifties America seemed to be abandoning manifested itself in several ways. To begin with, many craftspeople set up workshops away from the urban centers. Rural life seemed purer to them and more in keeping with the spirit of their enterprise. If country life proved

The Oriental simplicity of *Touch Sensitive,* a low-fire ceramic by Marvin Bjurlin, evokes similarly inspired 1950s pieces.

Marguerite Wildenhain's sturdy, stoneware held its own throughout the fifties, against a constant background of giggles coming from the giftware market where soulful craft items were mass-produced and the whole notion of "handmade" turned into a travesty.

Art by Marvin Bjurlin

Courtesy of The Brooklyn Museum

American Craft Council

unworkable, there was always the possibility of teaching at a design school or college, where one could absent oneself from the competitive "rat race" of midcentury American capitalism. Unlike the painters whose canvases were soon sporting hefty price tags, most craftspeople could not support themselves with their own work, and teaching afforded them financial security. As for financial success, that was not supposed to matter to the true craftsperson. Indeed, as Wildenhain noted, the true craftperson's life had to be one "dedicated to an idea that is not based on success and money, but on human independence and dignity."

Finally, this quest for purity was reflected, not only in a pure lifestyle, but in the actual objects that were created, many of which featured pure, unadorned forms. As is the case with so many designs of the 1950s, it is impossible to trace the simple appearance of these pieces back to any single influential source. The austerely geometric wall hangings of Anni Albers, for example, bespoke both the no-frills late Bauhaus aesthetic that embraced the machine age which seemed so threatening to crafts, as well as a back-to-basics attitude that saw handicrafts as a humanizing foil to increasing mechanization (this, an expression of the *early* Bauhaus viewpoint). Robert Turner's equally pure-looking, high-fired stoneware, on the other hand, did not hark back to the Bauhaus but to primitive pottery and Japanese ceramics. James Prestini's turned wooden bowls, with their slender walls and delicate edges, also evoked Oriental and tribal art. Marguerite Wildenhain's own pots displayed a Bauhaus influence (both she and Albers had studied there), as well as a solid, earthy quality very much in keeping with her own philosophy.

Although these craftspeople produced pieces similar in their purity, they would not necessarily have offered the same rationale for doing so. It seems clear, however, that all these pieces conveyed a single message of a simplicity and purity that stood in contrast to the growing complexity and rampant consumerism of American life at this time.

"Owning things corrupts one," declared weaver Anni Albers, who created the framed wall hanging *Tikal* in 1958. While Americans were not apt to share this sentiment, there was a devoted group of uncorrupted people who hailed the Bauhaus-trained emigré as a leader of the American crafts movement. Albers's wall hangings are now pricey collector's items.

Surface Brilliance

Beatrice Wood's luster-ware is best appreciated when viewed in the round, where one can see the continual play of light across its surfaces.

While fifties America was reveling in the high-gloss, two-tone finishes of its monster cars and painting the walls of its living rooms in harsh, garish tones, many craftspeople were creating objects that showed a softer sensitivity to surface texture and color. This, too, was seen as a means of introducing the human touch into what craftspeople perceived as a dehumanized and dehumanizing environment. Unlike those craftspeople who favored pure forms, however, these men and women chose to appeal to Americans in the fifties with luscious hues and vivid, unusual textures.

This approach is seen in a variety of crafts objects from that time. There were potters such as Beatrice Wood who created many pieces of gorgeously colored, iridescent lusterware; and the husband-and-wife team of Gertrude and Otto Natzler, who developed superb, subtly hued glazes for their delicately proportioned ceramic pieces, including the well-known "lava" glazes.

The handwoven carpets of Gerald Mast and Al Herbert for V'Soske featured brilliant colors and vivid textural contrasts within single pieces. All these craftspeople attempted to make objects that, in their visual or tactile richness, would elicit the kind of sensual awareness in the viewer that fast-paced, overly cushioned yet blaring modern life was destroying. As Beatrice Wood observed (quoted by Lee Nordness in *Objects: U.S.A.*), "With more comfort than ever before, man can be dangerously lulled into accepting packaged thought." It was this brand of thought, and the packaged way of seeing that went with it, that she and other craftspeople opposed. And it was this opposition that became concrete and substantial in their craftwork.

If some craftspeople saw color and texture as providing a relief from bland or overly slick mass-produced items, others appropriated those very qualities and used them for their own ends. For instance, Ed Rossbach took mass-produced materials like newspaper, plastic, and string and wove them into one-of-a-kind pieces. And there were those, like Dorothy Liebes, who brought hand-weaving and mass production together in richly textured, vibrantly hued handmade fabrics that were made partly with natural and partly with synthetic fibers. Poor Dorothy, critics would say. She weaves with garbage—at least that was what the gossips of the time were proclaiming. In fact, her textiles are among the most exciting of the decade.

American design of the fifties is loaded with paradoxes, and this interest on the part of craftspeople in richly colored and textured surfaces is one of them. The style favored by vanguard designers and architects of the decade tended toward reductionism—a restrained use of color, no ornamentation, and sharp, hard edges. And yet many of the craft objects of the period were extremely colorful and rather shaggy-looking. Indeed, Modern interiors often included such objects. For if these craft objects were conceived as a relief from impersonal, mass-produced ones, they also ended up offering relief from the notoriously "cold" look of fifties Modern design.

Theorem hese handwoven blinds by Dorothy Liebes bespeak this imaginative craftswoman's love of gaudy colors and metallic yarns. Unlike many craft objects of the fifties, those of Liebes exude some of the irrepressible high spirits that characterized American roadside architecture, and buildings by such architects as Bruce Goff and Frank Lloyd Wright.

Weaver Ed Rossbach was even more daring than Dorothy Liebes in the materials he chose to work with. Unlike Liebes, however, he has never made serious inroads into the mass-production arena. This woven screen was crafted in early 1950 of blackout and packing paper, silk yarn, and reed.

Abstract expressionist art aroused much greater interest on the part of the public and the critics than crafts did during the 1950s. And so, not surprisingly, some craftspeople viewed abstract expressionism with distaste. As the weaver Anni Albers said at the First Annual Conference of American Craftsmen in 1957, ''Whether it be sand or feathers, what is important to realize is, I think, that a material and its own characteristic resistance to treatment helps objectify the role of the one who works with it. Perhaps it is this lack of such material obstinacy. . .that is, in part, responsible for today's vogue of emotional introspection as dominant source material, in painting, for instance.''

Despite the disapproval of Albers and like-minded colleagues, many craftspeople of the 1950s found the abstract expressionist style entirely acceptable and proceeded to mine that particular vein in their own work. If there was a question in many people's minds as to whether the typical hand-crafted object was actually fine art or merely functional, the abstract expressionist craft pieces may have provided an answer. For as often as not, these gnarled, brutal-looking objects had no function at all but were, as in the work of Peter Voulkos and Rudy Autio, pieces of ceramic sculpture. ''When you are experimenting on the wheel, there are a lot of things you cannot explain,'' Voulkos declared, sounding more like the painters of his day than a craftsman. ''You just say to yourself, 'the form will find its way'—it always does. That's what makes it exciting.

Expressionism

These bumpy-textured ceramic tiles—typically ''fifties primitive''—are part of a tiled fireplace that Jean Nison created for the conference room in New York City's Lever House.

The minute you feel you understand what you are doing, it loses that searching quality."

Voulkos's sentiments are reminiscent of those voiced by abstract expressionist painters. But while painting was a male-dominated movement, crafts, traditionally the domain of women, had its female abstract ex-pressionists, too. The wall hangings created by Mariska Karasz, for example, often had a tempestuous quality about them. Certainly no one was going to mistake them for anything as mundane and useful as a tablecloth or blanket. The monumentally scaled tapestries of Lenore Tawney also had an unconcealed air of angst about them, which alternated with an equally unbridled rapture set off by the glories of a nature untouched by industrialization.

It is true, though, as Albers pointed out, that these craftspeople were faced with far more complex technical challenges than their painter counterparts. In their work, emotionalism is in some ways tempered by an obviously high degree of sheer skill. Karasz, for instance, handled embroidery and hand-dying in equally virtuoso fashion, while Voulkos had a reputation for being remarkably dextrous at the potter's wheel. Whether such skills enhanced the emotionalism, detracted from it, or were simply more interesting is a question of personal taste.

While debate over whether or not craft objects were fine art continued throughout the 1950s, craftspeople were continually borrowing visual motifs and themes from artists, and not the other way around. Some called this cross-fertilization, but it was pretty much a one-way street. This was evident in the abstract expressionist craft objects as well as in objects that featured figurative images. The New York School painters inspired the former; the latter turned for inspiration to the work of such well-known artists as Pa-

Figuratively Speaking

blo Picasso, Joan Miró, and Paul Klee. The techniques these craftspeople used in making their objects were often remarkably innovative, or else brilliant revivals of half-forgotten processes which they reinitiated. The end products, however, usually looked derivative. Enamelist Karl Drerup, glassmaker Edris Eckhardt, and the ceramicists Leza McVey and Edwin and Mary Scheier all appear to have derived at least some of their imagery from those of the above-mentioned painters. There was the same fascination with imprecisely drawn forms that had both self-consciously childlike and primitive qualities. In view of the fact that many of the craftspeople working in the United States at this time had emigrated from Europe with the rise of the Nazis, it is understandable that the influence of European Modern art would be evident in their American work. And with all the attention Modern art was getting in the press and in books, it follows that native American

craftspeople would be interested, too.

These craft objects inspired by Picasso, Miró, and Klee were far more affordable than a real Klee, Miró, or Picasso work; they attracted those people who were drawn to crafts and also those who were in no position to buy "the real thing." On the other hand, these pieces were not opportunistic imitations of inspired originals. For there was something refreshing about finding high-art imagery associated not with museum pieces but with objects intended for people's homes. If the craftspeople who employed it were, in a sense, stealing from so-called fine artists, they were also taking some of the pretentiousness out of that fine art, merely by using its themes in everyday objects that were not accorded the same reverence as paintings. In this, they were doing the opposite of the abstract expressionist craftspeople, who in their work seemed to aspire to the supposedly higher, more serious level of painting and sculpture. What's more, the objects inspired by Modern artists might also be seen as replacing a more stodgy kind of decorative art, that is, the bronze, marble, and plaster statuettes and ornate pottery figurines that had cluttered up American interiors since the late 1800s. Derivative as these newer craft objects may have been, they also had a fresh, unpretentious look to them that was a welcome alternative to the likes of Dresden shepherdesses, plaster cupids, and porcelain fairies.

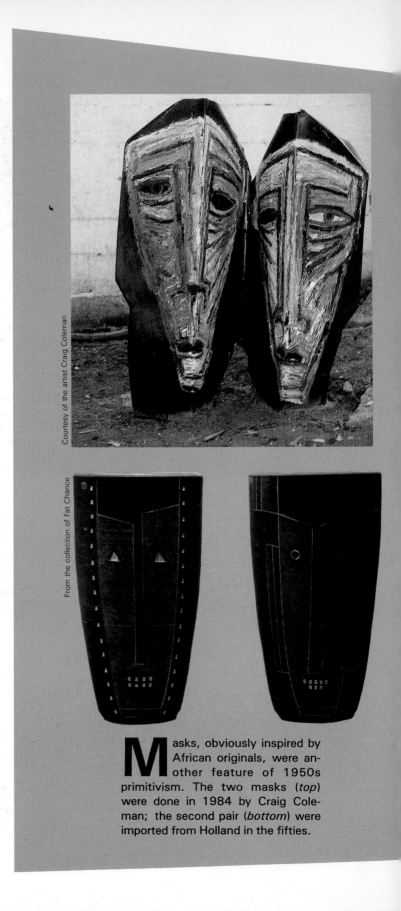

Courtesy of the artist Craig Coleman

From the collection of Fat Chance

Masks, obviously inspired by African originals, were another feature of 1950s primitivism. The two masks (*top*) were done in 1984 by Craig Coleman; the second pair (*bottom*) were imported from Holland in the fifties.

Pa Pa Piece (right), created by Philip Maberry in 1984, features the sort of freely drawn personage who appeared in countless guises in fifties ceramics. Compare, however, Maberry's piece with the one to its left. The fifties original seems more soulful, as was only appropriate at a time when craftspeople felt that they were preserving the very notion of "The Soul" in a soulless, hedonistic, conformist country.

The scratchily drawn woman's face on the surface of this Peter Voulkos piece (left) is the sort of thing that figured in numerous ceramics of the 1950s. Enterprising fifties lamp manufacturers had their designers rip off such motifs and stick them on the mass-produced ceramic bases of table lamps.

The Shape of Things

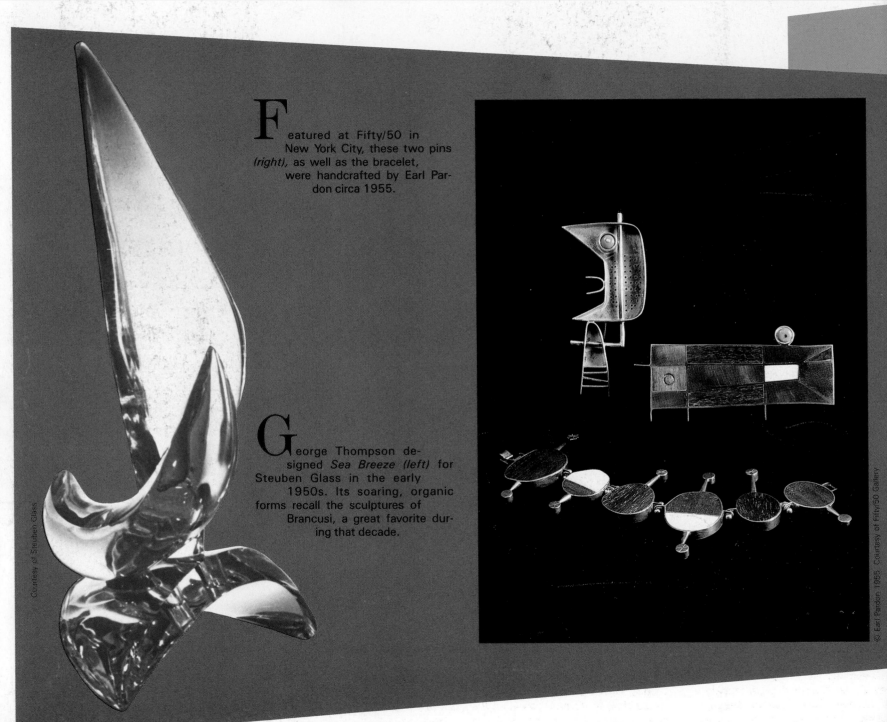

Featured at Fifty/50 in New York City, these two pins *(right)*, as well as the bracelet, were handcrafted by Earl Pardon circa 1955.

George Thompson designed *Sea Breeze (left)* for Steuben Glass in the early 1950s. Its soaring, organic forms recall the sculptures of Brancusi, a great favorite during that decade.

Courtesy of Steuben Glass

© Earl Pardon 1955. Courtesy of Fifty/50 Gallery

A friend of Jan de Swart's who worked at Dow Chemical during the fifties furnished the Los Angeles craftsman with samples of newly developed plastics even before they hit the market. With these, de Swart created colorful, bloboid sculptures like this one.

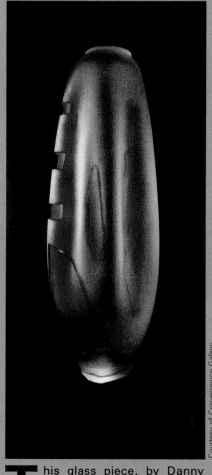

This glass piece, by Danny Perkins, recalls de Swart's organic plastic sculptures. Perkins's pieces are available from Convergence Gallery.

...f both abstract expressionist and figurative craft objects of the 1950s often derived from the art of the period, other pieces boasted a higher degree of originality. In most cases, these motifs were abstract and geometric, and they displayed a sense of joy in pattern for its own sake, without the overheated emotionalism of the expressionists or the occasionally too-cute,

pseudo-primitive personages favored by the figurists. This love of pattern was evident in the art fabrics of Sue Fuller, with their intricate, curvilinear webs of nylon monofilaments, and in the boldly patterned vessels of Maija Grotell, which were decorated with stylized flower, starburst, arc, and amoeba shapes, and in the swirls of Maurice Heaton's glass pieces.

In addition to abstract decorative motifs, many craft objects of the fifties were nonfunctional, abstract (though not abstract expressionist) forms, often with an organic flavor to them. Here abstraction was not used as a vehicle for presenting one's emotions through a visual medium. Rather, it was the abstract forms of nature that the craftsperson chose to evoke,

whether in glass (as in the "studies in crystal" created by the glassmakers at Steuben in the mid-1950s) or plastic (as in the unique work of Jan de Swart). These pieces came very close to sculpture. Their being labeled as crafts probably owes more to arbitrary distinctions about what materials a "serious" sculptor should use than to any aesthetic criteria.

American craft objects of the fifties were certainly not created with a mass market in mind. "It is the province of the craftsman to satisfy the demands of the discerning few," stated Jay Doblin of the Institute of Design at the Illinois Institute of Technology at the First Annual Conference of American Craftsmen in 1957. "Crafts should replace the appalling souvenir and gift markets," Doblin continued, referring to the mass-produced ceramics and assorted *objets* that were making their way into many working- and middle-class American homes at this time. "These are the worst possible areas of American production."

While many craftspeople did create for the discerning few—weaver Lenore Tawney, at the same conference, went so far as to say that "when you work, you must please yourself completely"—there were others who felt the desire to reach a wider public and who therefore designed not simply out of a need for self-expression and self-fulfillment, but to please consumers and make a living. Indeed, Rose Slivka, editor-in-chief of the influential *Craft Horizons* magazine, in her introduction to Julie Hall's *Tradition and Change: The New American Craftsman*, declared that far from being elitist, crafts were ideal art objects for an egalitarian society because they were affordable to more than just the ruling class. And so, while many craftspeople were content to sell their work themselves and through galleries, others attempted to market what they did on a larger scale.

One of the most successful of these was the weaver Dorothy Liebes. By the

Marketing Craft Objects

Dorothy Liebes wove shimmery threads of Lur*(right)*, a plastic-coated metal yarn first manufactured in t fifties by Dobeckmun, into this theater curtain. Fifties tast makers called Lurex tacky, but Liebes is said to have endow it with respectability.

These unusual pieces *(far right)* were manufactured Shawnee in the fifties. Faking the obvious was a hallmark some fifties fashion design, but these wood-grained c ramics from Beige Gallery stretch things a bit—no o would ever mistake them for real wood.

This fused enameled glass bowl, designed by Frances Higgins, is distinguished by delicate tracery in fawn and black.

American Craft Council

Michael Zapatello. Courtesy of Beige Gallery

ate fifties, Liebes was devoting all her energy to designing for industry, an activity she considered to be more in keeping with the democratic spirit of America than the weaving of expensive, one-of-a-kind pieces for a wealthy, international clientele that had occupied her earlier in the decade. Liebes adored bright colors, as an artist and as a businesswoman: ''Color, of course, is an all-important factor,'' she once observed, ''because it's the first thing to catch a shopper's eye.''

Other craftspeople in the fifties were also perfectly happy to join in with the more lucrative free enterprise of the times. Brian and Edith Heath, for example, working in Sausalito, California, had started out doing one-of-a-kind dinnerware pieces that were available on a limited basis at Gump's, the San Francisco department store. The pieces sold well, and demand for them increased to the point where only machine production allowed the Heaths to meet it. Glassmakers Frances and

Michael Higgins also enjoyed considerable financial success. Through a national distributor, they sold as many as fifteen thousand pieces a year. In 1952, along with three other artists, metalworker Ronald Hayes Pearson opened a shop in Rochester, New York, where his silver and gold pieces were quickly snapped up by customers, while Harold and Trudi Sitterle produced a line of graceful white porcelain tableware at their kilns in Croton Falls, New York, which were sold in

retail shops. The line was successful, but the Sitterles purposely limited production so that they could do it all themselves and thereby control all aspects of their work.

None of these craftspeople, however, was as successful as weaver Jack Lenor Larsen was in the fifties. Starting in the middle of the decade, Larsen set about building his own extremely lucrative international fabric, carpeting, and furniture empire, which thrives to this day.

Those pieces made by today's craftspeople that hark back to the fifties style refer to its kitschier aspects. In a sense, this is not so astounding, given the fact that even during the 1950s craftspeople often took their cue from developments in the so-called fine arts. Today, when a combination of intellectual and economic considerations has led to the creation of accessible works of art with popular appeal (albeit a popular appeal often spiced with a dash of irony), artists are looking toward the pop iconography of the 1950s for inspiration—and so are the craftspeople.

In keeping with this trend, craftspeople draw not upon the "highbrow" crafts of the fifties but rather upon its vernacular, particularly as manifested in such areas as textile design and roadside architecture. Boomerang and free-form shapes, jutting geometric forms, intentionally garish color combinations—all recall the sort of 1950s artifacts that never made it to the Museum of Modern Art and similarly hallowed strongholds of Modern

Hands On

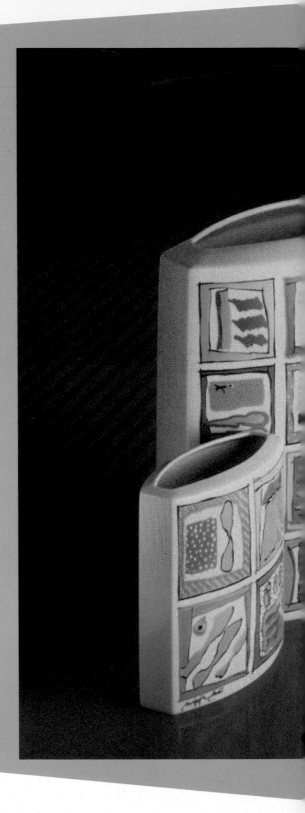

Dari Gordon's pot, made in 1982 and available through Convergence Gallery in New York City, recalls some fifties ceramics with its wavy-edged decorative motifs and pastel pink hue.

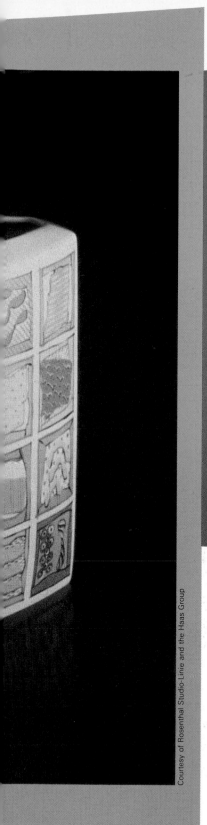

Dorothy Haffner's *Manhattan* vases *(left)*, designed for Rosenthal Studio-Linie, feature a pattern of freely drawn abstract motifs not unlike those that graced the ceramics, lamp bases, and graphic designs of the 1950s. The bouncy pastel colors, however, are very much of the eighties, with none of the dry earthiness of fifties hues. Still, they would work well with original fifties furniture as well as with any of today's fifties-inspired designs.

In some ways, the dreamlike figures depicted on this plate *(right)* by ceramist Ken Pick hark back to the commercialized surrealism of the 1950s. Pick's masterful, unrestrained use of color, on the other hand, would have been more or less unfamiliar to ceramists of the time, who kept color low-key.

design, though they certainly did make their owners feel as if they, too, were living in the modern age.

Today's craftspeople emphasize handwork, but in doing so they are by no means rejecting technology in the way many fifties craftspeople did. On the contrary, they celebrate fifties kitsch—the sort of plastic, synthetic stuff that often owed its very existence to the technology of mass production so many fifties craftspeople deplored or, at best, mistrusted. By doing so, they declare their acceptance (or at least amused tolerance) of the vagar-

ies of late twentieth-century America.

Today's 1950s-inspired craft objects differ from actual fifties pieces in their lack of practicality as well as in their spirit. In fact, many do not function at all but are meant to serve more as sculpture—a far cry from the fifties when, at least in those pieces made according to Modernist tenets, functionality took precedence over the merely decorative. For today's craftspeople working in fifties-related styles, an object can be not only politely whimsical or sophisticatedly childlike (characteristics of many 1950s crafts

pieces) but downright funny, campy, brash, and exuberant. At the same time, these craftspeople are aware that such works are not so much in keeping with the mood of these tense times as they are an ironic comment on them.

It should be noted that along with the younger craftspeople whose work is fifties-influenced, a number of men and women whose pieces became well-known *during* the 1950s are still at work today. In many cases, their recent creations can be seen as further steps along lines they were beginning to explore in the fifties.

4

Furniture and Furnishings

Like most periods of furniture design, the 1950s has its classics. These are the pieces that tastemakers, historians, museum curators, and design cognoscenti deem beyond fashion's dictates, enshrining them in that pantheon where standards remain fixed for all eternity. The design classics of the fifties, all agree, are seminal pieces, some designed by Charles Eames in collaboration with his wife, Ray; others created by George Nelson and manufactured by the Herman Miller Co.; and the equally significant

"Good Design"

pieces created by Eero Saarinen, Harry Bertoia, and Florence Schust Knoll (now Bassett) for Knoll Associates.

These pieces are classics, in fact, not so much of design but of *Modern* design. The distinction ought to be made. As will be seen from the following pages, furniture of similarly high caliber was being designed in the United States at the same time that these pieces appeared on the market. That the former failed to assume classic status has less to do with their intrinsic value than it has to do with the powerful dictators of fashion at that time.

The taste of the time, at least among certain influential designers, ran along more or less the same lines as that of the Bauhaus in its final phase, before it was forced to close by the Nazis. In Germany after World War I, the architects and designers of the Bauhaus had theorized that simple, functional, unornamented, massproduced furniture, designed accord-

ing to the principles of industrial technology and priced to be affordable to as many people as possible, would somehow lead to a better world. A school of fine and applied art, the Bauhaus boasted such faculty members as the architects Walter Gropius, Marcel Breuer, and Ludwig Mies van der Rohe. When the Bauhaus closed in the late thirties, several of its leading lights came to teach in American universities, where they espoused the tenets of Modern design.

At the time, Modern design was not yet understood or accepted in America. Popular taste in the 1930s tended toward reproductions of both American and European period pieces, or streamlined pieces that were futuristic in a playful but, some thought, superficial way. The only contemporary furniture that had met with any success at all was Finnish architect Alvar Aalto's laminated birch pieces, which people found warmer-looking than the tubular steel-and-chrome pieces favored at the Bauhaus. Later, in the fifties, Scandinavian design became a major influence in America, resulting in the "Danish Modern" style that is well known today.

Even before former Bauhaus faculty members and students came to America, however, interest in Modern design—both German and Scandinavian—had been growing. The Museum of Modern Art (MOMA) had been founded in 1929 in New York City; its directors were thoroughly familiar with the Bauhaus outlook and

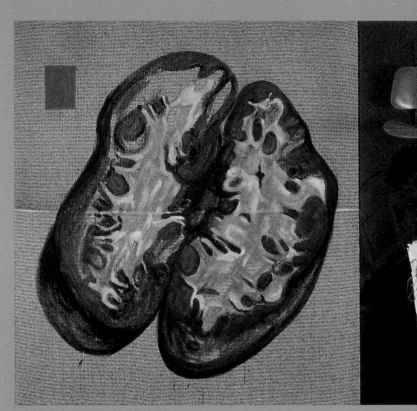

In his 1983 painting *Brother Animal (right)*, artist David Salle, a great admirer of fifties designs, made the Eames LCW chair seem more organic than ever by juxtaposing two legless ones with what looks like a sliced-open kidney or liver.

In their notes for an exhibition of Charles Eames and Ray Kaiser Eames's designs held at their gallery, Fifty/50 in New York City, Mark McDonald, Mark Isaacson, and Ralph Cutler note that the 1946 red all-wood low chair (LCW) also came in a yellow and a blue version that were never put into production. During the 1950s, The Herman Miller Company did, however, manufacture the same chair with the red stain, the black stain, and with natural wood finishes.

With today's Interest In residential interior design, we are apt to forget that Modern furniture of the 1950s, with which people now are furnishing their homes, was often meant as furniture for public and work places. The crisp-lined desk and the desk-and-wall unit were designed by George Nelson for the Herman Miller Company.

were impressed enough to want to convey it to the American public. But perhaps "impressed" is not a strong enough word. Modern design (with that capital "M") became a sort of gospel truth. To these men and women, it was not a question of mere aesthetics, not a matter of their liking the way Modern design *looked*. For them, it was what design had to be. Period.

Throughout the latter half of the 1930s, MOMA held several "Useful Objects" exhibits to introduce Americans to functional, mass-produced, well-designed, and sensibly priced household items. By the early 1940s, however, it became clear that notwithstanding the useful household objects already available, Americans needed more good Modern furniture. In response to this need, over the next decade, MOMA, in conjunction with like-minded retailers and manufacturers, held several design competitions to stimulate the creation of low-cost and "organic" furniture, lamps, textiles, and playground equipment, among other items. The winning designs were to go into mass production and eventually be sold throughout the country.

The Museum of Modern Art and its collaborators were not alone in wanting to promote Modern design in America. Several other manufacturers, most notably the Herman Miller Co. and Knoll Associates, were also drawn to it. Embracing the utopian aims and new production techniques favored by Modern design, these manufacturers developed and produced furniture created by American designers (Knoll also produced several Bauhaus pieces by Breuer and Mies).

The American designers involved with both MOMA and the manufacturers—among them the Eameses, Saarinen, Knoll, Nelson, and Bertoia—created furniture in which Bauhaus and twentieth-century Scandinavian design aesthetics were combined. Scandinavian design, already familiar to some Americans thanks to the Aalto furniture that had been imported from Finland since the thirties, emphasized both handcrafting *and* industrial technology. It was, however, at the Cranbrook Academy in Bloomfield Hills, Michigan, that many of these designers became steeped in the Scandinavian design aesthetic. Founded in 1932, the philosophy of this design school called for an integrated approach to all aspects of design and influenced young designers as strongly as did that of the Bauhaus. Following the example of both the Bauhaus and the Scandinavian designers, the Americans experimented with new production methods and new materials, such as plastics and plywood laminates molded into three dimensions, in an effort to mass-produce well-designed furniture.

Production of this furniture had hardly gotten under way when World War II began. For the duration of the war, all industrial research, including that which had gone on in the furniture industry, was geared toward the military. Designer Charles Eames, working for the U.S. Navy, used his previous knowledge of wood laminating and molding to develop a splint. In turn, many of the technological advances made during the war—especially in the aircraft industry—were to be applied to furniture design once the war was over.

When the war ended, the prevailing mood in victorious America was one of optimism. Americans approached life with new enthusiasm. In this spirit, it seemed as if a sizable public might prove receptive to the furniture that had begun to be developed in the 1940s and was now being produced and sold. What better way to confirm the new era than to furnish homes in a completely new style? The cry was what it had once been at the Bauhaus: simple, rational furniture for a simple, rational world. The response to this hue and cry was Modern American design.

As postwar prosperity increased, classics flowed from both the Herman Miller Co. and Knoll in a steady stream. Eames plywood chairs (1946) and plastic shell chairs (1949), Eames storage units (1950), wire side chairs (1951), lounge chair and ottoman (1956), and the aluminum group (1958), designed for Miller, all met with an enthusiastic response from Modern designers and those in sympathy with their outlook. The press, too, was most enthusiastic. George Nelson's furniture, including several innovative storage systems, had a less identifiable style than the Eames's pieces, though they too offered new, unusual, and occasionally humorous approaches to design. Knoll commissioned designs from architect Eero Saarinen, the most notable of which were his "Womb" chair (1948) and

"Pedestal" tables and chairs (1955-1957), and from sculptor Harry Bertoia, whose chairs of welded steel latticework were first introduced in 1952. While claiming to have designed "fill in" pieces that no one else wanted to take on, Florence Knoll (who had married Hans Knoll, the company's founder, and assumed leadership over it when her husband was killed in a car crash), created chairs, tables, desks and case goods, many of them incorporating steel-supporting parts, with severe forms and luxurious materials.

Though these pieces did not always resemble one another, they were all alike in their skillful incorporation of new materials and manufacturing techniques and in their cool, almost austere quality. As Saarinen himself said, if mass-produced pieces were to be true to the spirit of the industrial age, they "must never lose their im-

Courtesy of Herman Miller, Inc.

The Eames *Lounge Chair and Ottoman (left)* is considered by many to be the most comfortable Modern chair ever designed. The Herman Miller Company still manufactures this down-filled classic.

Critic Russell Lynes considered this lamp *(top right)*, designed by Kurt Versen in the late forties and popular throughout the 1950s, to be the epitome of "highbrow" taste. Made of black metal tubing with a burlap shade, it can be found at the Beige Gallery in New York City.

Like Charles Eames, George Nelson also designed furniture for the Herman Miller Company, including the *Coconut* chair *(bottom right)*, found today in shops that carry fifties "antiques."

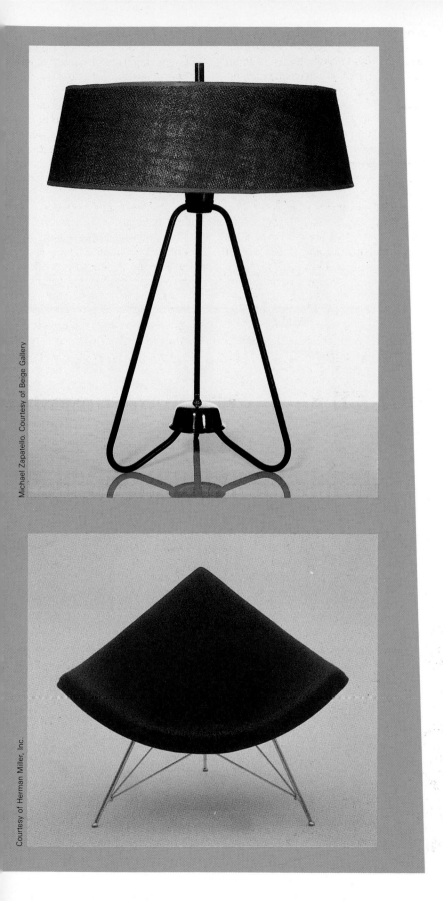

personal character.'' But it was not merely a question of a piece of furniture's *looking* up-to-date and impersonal. That impersonality, due to the lack of both ornamentation and any relationship to earlier, familiar design styles, carried with it a moral message. As D. J. De Pree, the guiding entrepreneurial force behind the Herman Miller Co., stated, ''We came to believe that faddish styles and early obsolescence are forms of immorality. . . . By good design, I mean design that is simple and honest. . . . Things should look like what they are, with no fakery, no finishes to simulate the patina of age, and no surface embellishment other than the material itself properly finished.'' And so, for example, if Eames joined a molded plastic shell to a metal leg to make a chair, the points where plastic and metal joined were to be exposed, not hidden. Similarly, if a chair was in fact made of plastic, the plastic was supposed to *look* like plastic and not malachite or leather or any other, possibly more expensive material. During the 1950s many critics, designers, and architects hailed this new design philosophy. Some, however, had their doubts, like Russell Lynes, who in his book *The Tastemakers* suggested that ''honest design'' was just another public relations ploy.

Considerable energy went into promoting the new Modern design in the late forties and early fifties. Impetus was given to the movement by the ever-supportive Museum of Modern Art, where several ''Good Design'' exhibitions, similar to the Useful Objects shows of the thirties, presented the public with the best in Modern design. The exhibitions were shown at both MOMA and the Chicago Merchandise Mart, where they introduced buyers from department and home-furnishings stores across America to Modern design. Some department stores sold the pieces featured in these exhibitions, and MOMA helped attract customers by providing retailers with plans and materials with which to set up Good Design displays in their own stores. With or without a Good Design promotional campaign, several department stores across the country offered Modern furniture, as did numerous specialty shops that sold ''contemporary'' pieces. Design magazines touted the furniture, and everyone from MOMA to architects to home economics teachers insisted that this fresh, new, exciting style was the best style in which to furnish a home.

However, it seemed, at least in the fifties, that even if certain authorities praised a design, the majority of consumers would not necessarily agree with them. Indeed, it soon became clear that what had been intended, at least in theory, as affordable, high-quality design for the masses was nothing of the sort. It was true that some designers were creating modern furniture for people's homes (see pages 84-85). But the classics of this period—some of which were by no means cheap—appealed not so much to homeowners or apartment dwellers but to the architects and other designers who held Modernism in such high esteem. Indeed, Knoll never made its furniture available to anyone *but* architects and designers, who at the time were targeted as the firm's most likely customers. And only *some* of the Miller pieces were sold in department and furniture stores. Despite all the brouhaha, it was ultimately in the exclusive private homes and public buildings that architects designed that the Modern classics found their proper place. Indeed, once it had become clear that the largest market for Modern American furniture was corporate and commercial rather than residential, much of it was designed specifically with offices, and not homes, in mind.

Today there is no reason to doubt the quality of these classic designs. But to view them as *the* designs of the 1950s is to deny the variety of furniture design of those years. History tells us that the fifties saw the uncontested triumph of Modern design in America. Certainly Modern furniture became *the* office furniture in those years. But parallel and equally important developments were occurring at the same time, often in opposition to the tenets of Modernism. Though they were less widely promoted, they are nevertheless worthy of the attention the classics received and continue to receive.

While the American design classics of the fifties fulfilled the Bauhaus and Scandinavian ideals of functionality, many of them were actually quite expensive (several of the Eames chairs being notable exceptions). However, once the Modernist spirit had caught on, a number of other designers also created furniture for manufacturers eager to capture a larger, style-conscious—if somewhat less affluent—market. These designers shared the outlook of the Eameses, Saarinen, Nelson, Knoll, and Bertoia but were looked spare enough; but made as they were of luxurious woods, chromed metal, and marble, they were not the sort of thing a young couple just starting out could afford. Designers of less expensive pieces, on the other hand, eschewed luxury entirely. Intended for the "Young Moderns" ("this always meant young-couples-on-a-budget," designer Milo Baughman recalls), the pieces were stripped to the bare essentials. The furniture was lightweight and spindly-looking, and it was often set on the skinny

Cost Effective

willing to use relatively inexpensive materials to keep the price low. The Museum of Modern Art, in an effort to make Modern design more widely available, had sponsored a low-cost furniture design competition between 1947 and 1950, the winners of which included plastic shell armchairs and side chairs by Charles and Ray Eames. Likewise, in MOMA's 1950 lamp design competition, the price of the items, though not a decisive factor, was to be kept "within reasonable limits." And, as mentioned previously, the museum had held exhibitions featuring examples of what its staff judged to be well-designed, reasonably priced household items. With all this, MOMA set a trend, for many other furniture manufacturers soon became interested in producing low-cost Modern furniture.

The low-cost furniture that eventually flooded the market was strictly functional, with no frills whatsoever. Florence Knoll's pieces may have wrought-iron legs with matte black finish that in time became synonymous with the popular idea of Modern design. Inexpensive hardwoods like maple, birch, and ash were used. Tight seats and backs were common, because they required less fabric and less labor. All in all, the furniture had a clean, trim, informal look that seemed to bespeak the postwar way of life. In its often absolute rectilinearity, it recalled the severe and very abstract compositions of the Dutch painter Piet Mondrian.

Big, cushiony club chairs and sofas did not figure into this scheme. Boxy, somewhat up-to-date-looking, reasonably priced upholstered pieces were being produced. But, as Sharon Darling pointed out in *Chicago Furniture*, these "lacked what many young architects and designers considered to be 'good design.'" While plump reclining chairs caught the fancy of young suburbanites—it was just the thing for dad after a hard day's work at the

Conran's offers the *Slim* chair *(above)*, whose black wrought-iron frame resembles the more austere Modern furniture of the fifties. The candy-striped seat, on the other hand, lends it a "fun" aspect much perkier than the wry humor of most 1950s fabrics.

Milo Baughman's light-looking Modern pieces *(right)* were created for Pacific Iron in 1950. Their sleek lines make them thoroughly appropriate for spacious eighties interiors.

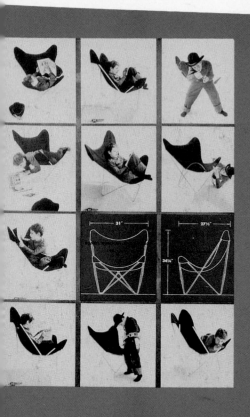

Knoll's brilliant series *(left)* of advertisements for furniture during the fifties often had a dry witty quality. This one for the Hardoy—a.k.a. *Butterfly*—chair was no exception.

Gary Falk's 1982 painting *(right)*, enameled acrylic on aluminum, presents a rebus of a running bunny, an exploding ring, a grid, and a 1950s Butterfly chair.

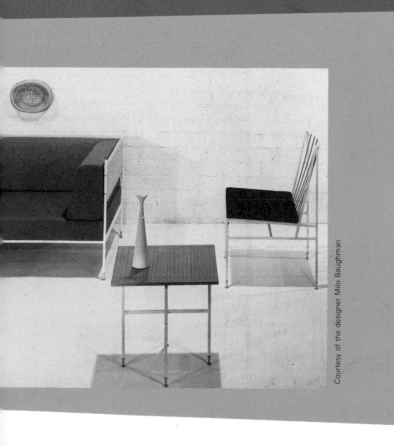

office, said the ads—the better-designed, affordable Modern pieces included chairs and sofas with crisp, upholstered foam pads that were set about four inches off the floor on slightly splayed wooden or metal legs. This furniture, created by such designers as Paul McCobb, Milo Baughman, and the Los Angeles design team of Hendrik Van Keppel and Taylor Green, was meant to be light enough to be moved by housewives who had no servants to shift things around for them when it came time to vacuum the living room. What's more, it boasted an airy, open appearance that made it an ideal space-saver for the sort of modestly scaled living quarters newlyweds in the early fifties were able to afford. Chairs folded and occasional tables either stacked or nested into one another—another way to cut down the amount of floor space pieces required. Quite apart from its practicality, this furniture conferred a certain status on its owners, and showed them to be thoroughly up-to-the-minute in their tastes. Finally, unlike the more costly classics, which were supposedly *the* furniture of the fifties, these Modern pieces were widely available—and were the ones that people bought. By the mid-1950s, however, these strictly functional pieces began to fall from favor. People considered them too transient-looking. Affordable though they were, they did not suggest the comforts of home; and by the middle of the decade, with American prosperity at its peak, comfort was something all felt entitled to. The furniture that continued to be designed in this style was primarily for outdoor use. The only piece that remained extremely popular for interiors as well was the Hardoy chair. Originally introduced by Knoll, it spawned countless imitations. Also known as the "Butterfly" chair, it remains popular—and cheap—to this day.

While designers of both the classics and the more affordable Modern furniture made a sharp break with past styles, other American designers of the 1950s tried to effect a compromise with earlier styles. These designers updated forms from the past, and many of their pieces blended in perfectly with older furniture. Their work met with a warm response from some quarters. As one *House Beautiful* editor exulted in 1953, "The battle between modern and traditional is over. And we the people have won! . . . So

the furniture that these people wanted to live with, although they considered it fine for the office.

It was radicalness *and* unfamiliarity of Modern furniture that put Middle Americans off. At the height of the Red Scare, in 1951, another *House Beautiful* editor proclaimed that "Americans like Modern furniture, but it's our own Modern, never cold, foreign, or austere." Of course neither Knoll nor the Herman Miller Co. were run by communists; nor could the influences in the furniture they manufactured be in

A Sense of the Past

the negation of modern design—the stripped-down look, the stubborn rejection of all ornament, the frigid, fixed forms—is yielding with grace to the long-suppressed desire for enrichment. So, too, the equally negative stubbornness of traditional design is reasonably giving way to the needs of contemporary life for beauty *plus performance*, character *plus comfort*." In fact, no such clear-cut victory had been reached. Try as they might, magazine editors could not make total sense of things, and countertrends kept on moving in divergent directions.

Still, there certainly was a market for this kind of design, especially among the more affluent homeowners of Middle America who subscribed to such shelter magazines as *House Beautiful* and *House & Garden,* both of which ran a great deal of it during the 1950s. This sector of society had always had conservative taste in furniture. Though Modern design was causing a stir in the fifties, it was not

any way traced to the Soviet Union or any of the fellow travelers who figured so prominently in McCarthyist demonology. Nevertheless, there must have been something vaguely socialistic and alien about the very form of Modern furniture that some Americans did not cotton to.

Aside from this, much Modern furniture had a lightweight, almost floating quality to it that gave people an impression of impermanence and insecurity. The Cold War and high-speed progress made some Americans feel nervous. Quasi-traditional furniture helped allay such nervousness. This is perhaps most evident in an amusing ad run by Dunbar, the company that manufactured the designs of Edward Wormley. In the ad, two astronauts are carrying a Wormley sofa onto the lunar surface, while the copy states, "We will always feel the same about our creature comforts whether we pitch our tent on the green hills or among the suns and the moons."

John Van Kort alluded to the classic American Windsor chair with this fifties design. Its clean lines and quirky details make it seem as fresh today as it did thirty years ago.

Frank Lloyd Wright designed this laminate pine dining ensemble, circa 1950, for Woodside in Marion, Indiana. When designing furniture, the architect rarely thought about the human form. Consequently, his chairs in particular tend to be not very comfortable, though they are visually impressive. These recall the early twentieth-century pieces of Charles Rennie Mackintosh.

Edward Wormley's interest in art nouveau design is evident in the whiplash curves of the dining chairs he designed for Dunbar in the mid-1950s. Wormley's furniture is always superbly crafted of rich materials, generously scaled, quietly stylish, and comfortable. For those reasons, it is well worth acquiring—quite apart from its value as an investment.

Although design historians tend to overlook this furniture, much of it is quite successful in the way it revived the past with respect and without saccharine sentimentality. George Nakashima, for example, although primarily a craftsperson, created a handful of pieces for machine production, including a dining chair that harked back to the Windsor chair of colonial America as well as to Shaker furniture. And Edward Wormley drew on Victorian and art nouveau sources as well as the designs of Louis Comfort Tiffany and John Soane for the luxurious pieces he created for Dunbar.

Other designers worked in this vein as well. Russel Wright's popularity peaked in the 1930s and 1940s, but in 1950 he came out with his "Easier Living" line of large-scaled but lightweight sycamore furniture that boasted reasonable prices and a plainspoken, vaguely traditional appearance that, if nothing else, must have struck people as wholesomely American. And in 1954 John van Kort presented his "Profile" collection that turned out to be a great money-maker for Drexel, blending as it did features reminiscent of contemporary Scandinavian design with a solid look people associated with traditional furniture. The Englishman T. H. Robsjohn-Gibbings was another designer who thought very much in terms of both the present and the past. In reviving neoclassical and Italianate motifs in his designs for John Widdicomb, he noted, in a 1955 issue of *House Beautiful,* that "it is beauty, in the oldest meaning of the word, that we are all searching for. . . . Unfortunately the past, where the beauty that will inspire us is waiting to be discovered, has been abused and ignored for the last 50 years." And while Frank Lloyd Wright was by no means a standard-bearer of traditional values, his towering architectural genius had become, by the 1950s, a tradition in and of itself. The furniture he designed for Henredon, though not very successful and said to be rather uncomfortable, did have a hefty appearance that appealed to some of those customers who sought a compromise between the modern and the familiar.

Way Out

Form follows function was the watchword for most Modern designers of the fifties. Others harked back to the past or drew their inspiration from Scandinavia. Along with these classics—the strictly functional, the Danish modern, and the neoconservative pieces—there was free-form furniture. Here Modernism took on a self-consciously futuristic, theatrical character. Honesty and simplicity did not figure into these designs. Form followed, not function, but the designer's fancy. As Erwine Laverne, who with his wife, Estelle, created some of the most unusual free-form pieces, stated, "The time you're being creative is when you're sleeping—if you're looking for logic, it escapes you." While the established tastemakers of the period might have looked askance at this philosophy, the furniture that resulted from it did delight a number of buyers.

Much free-form furniture was produced on a fairly limited scale and was never sold in the retail market. The Lavernes, for example, designed and manufactured their own furniture, selling it through their showrooms to both corporate and residential clients throughout America and Europe. Their molded fiberglass and clear plastic pieces tended to be large-scale, and they did not look like anything anyone had ever seen before, at least insofar as furniture went.

In fact, the free-form pieces designed by the Lavernes and others were not entirely *sui generis*. Some of the furniture designs coming out of Italy in the fifties resembled these American pieces in their exuberant,

Courtesy of Laverne Inc.

In the late 1950s, Laverne International offered the *Lotus* chair *(left)* in black or white molded fiberglass and the *Tulip* chair *(right)* in white fiberglass. They count as two of the most imaginative chair designs of that decade—and as wise investments today, when they are not easy to find.

unpredictable forms. And Aalvar Alto, in addition to favoring undulating forms in some of his buildings, had designed several unusual glass vases in the early 1930s whose shapes, reminiscent of Finland's fjords, may have served as an inspiration. The fantastic work of Antonio Gaudí was another possible inspiration.

It is true that the Eames 1949 molded plastic chair and the Saarinen ''Womb'' chair boasted free forms themselves. These forms, however, were arrived at only after careful consideration of manufacturing techniques and human posture and not out of a sense of whimsy. Their free forms were incidental to the fact that they functioned properly. True free-form furniture was not *un*-functional, but here form itself was the main point.

Perhaps the most immediate influence on free-form fifties furniture can be found in surrealist painting and sculpture: the melting watches of Salvador Dali, the blob-like rocks in Yves Tanguy's paintings, the amoeboid forms in the work of Hans (Jean) Arp. And, while surrealist artists drew heavily on the psychoanalytical technique of free association, the freedom free-form furniture expressed was not merely that of the unconscious but also of brashly optimistic postwar America itself, in which, thanks to a booming economy, all things seemed possible.

Vladimir Kagan also designed a good deal of free-form furniture at this time. Unlike the Lavernes, however, he worked mainly in wood. With fabric designer Hugo Dreyfuss, Kagan also created many massive, strangely shaped, upholstered pieces that were well-suited to the expansive spaces his well-to-do clients inhabited. There they could be positioned away from the wall and viewed, like sculpture, in the round. In fact, Kagan approached furniture design with a sculptor's sense of three-dimensionality and scale and

These plastic chairs from Rotocast Plastic Products suggest that fifties futurism is alive and well in the 1980s. Apart from an evocative appearance, their circular gaps make them the ideal armchair for small rooms.

Courtesy of Rotocast Plastic Products Inc.

Looking Out the Window Abstractly

Art by M. Louise Stanley. Courtesy of Quay Gallery.

Way out furniture for way out people: M. Louise Stanley's 1980 pencil drawing, entitled *Looking Out the Window Abstractly.*

Little is known about this curious piece of furniture—an end table/magazine rack/lamp—except for the fact that it was designed sometime between 1955 and 1959, is made of wood and string, and was never mass-produced. It embodies the sort of idiosyncratic, ruggedly individualistic, typically American inventiveness often seen in fifties commercial roadside architecture.

Today, it can be found at the Beige Gallery.

Michael Zapatello. Courtesy of Beige Gallery.

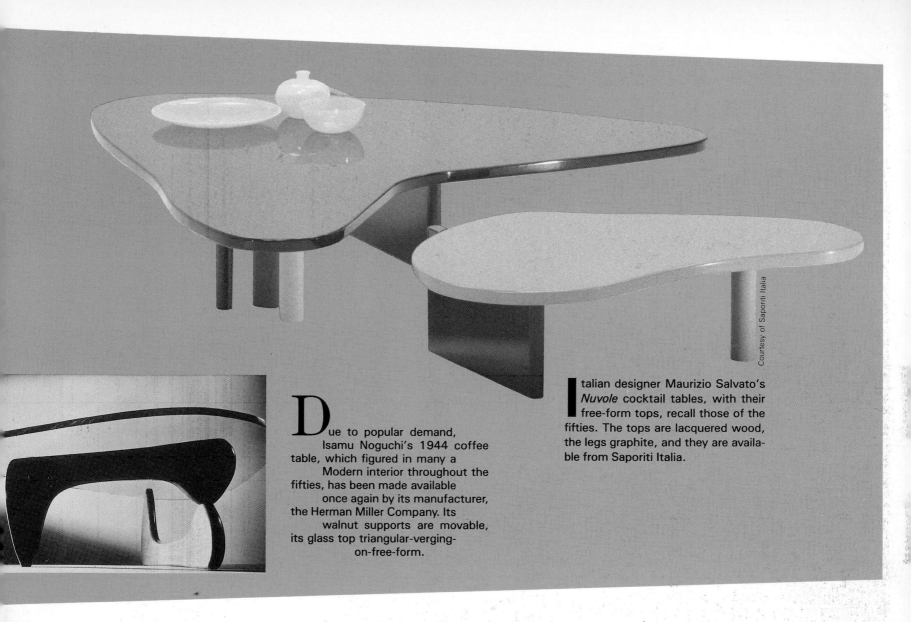

Italian designer Maurizio Salvato's *Nuvole* cocktail tables, with their free-form tops, recall those of the fifties. The tops are lacquered wood, the legs graphite, and they are available from Saporiti Italia.

Courtesy of Saporiti Italia

Due to popular demand, Isamu Noguchi's 1944 coffee table, which figured in many a Modern interior throughout the fifties, has been made available once again by its manufacturer, the Herman Miller Company. Its walnut supports are movable, its glass top triangular-verging-on-free-form.

with a craftsman's expertise. "Taking a metal tube and bending it into a chair was not what I wanted to do," he recalls. "I wanted to create my own imagery." Kagan's furniture was not only original; handcrafted as it was, it was also expensive.

Although the free-form pieces seem to have little to do with the technological innovations of Saarinen and the Eameses, their outlandish forms did in fact occasion certain new developments. For example, Kagan and Dreyfuss were obliged to develop and produce their own fabrics to wrap around the foam rubber shapes of the furniture. As for the Lavernes, they invented their own techniques for manufacturing their line of "invisible" plastic furniture.

If people were not eager to furnish their homes entirely with free-form furniture (its abundant *joie de vivre* automatically disqualified it for offices), the free-form *look*—for example, in the guise of a cocktail table—was acceptable as a foil for more sober pieces. Giddy from a highball, on what better surface could someone put his glass than a giddily curvaceous piece of free-form furniture? Sculptor Isamu Noguchi designed such a cocktail table for the Herman Miller Co., with a glass top and movable base. Jens Ri-

som, the Danish designer working in New York City, created one in wood. Rather conservative in most of his designs, T. H. Robsjohn-Gibbings let himself go when it came to cocktail tables, creating several of the amoebalike, free-form variety.

Middle America did not entirely ignore the free-form aesthetic. Indeed, some of its denizens were willing to accent their living rooms with free-form patterned fabrics (see Patterns, page 94), and drive up to roadside restaurants, bowling alleys, and motels that featured some very free forms. But while amoeboid or palette-shaped cocktail and end tables were

fun, and sectional sofas with serpentine edges thoroughly acceptable, anything more outlandish struck people as not being furniture. In the late 1950s, designers Robert and Anne Gera created a free-form line for S. Karpen and Bros., a Chicago manufacturer, that was meant to reach "the sophisticated 10 percent" of the residential market, a fraction of all consumers, true, but a larger number than had ever been able to buy pieces made by the Lavernes or Kagan. Unfortunately the line did not sell well. Apparently Americans wanted club chairs that *looked* like club chairs, not like something out of a sci-fi spaceship.

While handweavers in the fifties were exploiting texture for its sheer visual beauty and expressive qualities, textile designers were creating highly textured fabrics—using both natural and synthetic fibers—and carpeting for both residential and commercial interiors. They did so for a variety of reasons that ranged from the functional to the spiritual.

To begin with the spiritual, many vanguard designers of the decade believed, in accordance with both Bauhaus and Modernist tenets, that structure and materials should be expressed in every design. This frank acknowledgment of the technology that made the chair possible and the materials of which it was made was seen as a kind of honesty, which would result in a visually pleasing piece of furniture—and in a morally commendable one. Similarly, by making the weave of a fabric visible, one was choosing to conceal neither its material nor its mode of manufacture. The wish implicit in such a design philosophy went something like this: honest furniture will somehow make the people who sit in it more honest, too, and thereby bring about a better, harmonious world.

The paradox here is that if unconcealed machine technology gave furniture a blunt, industrial look, fabrics woven on power looms tended to have an overly refined quality that these vanguard designers detested. And so, in the fifties, to make a fabric look more honest—that is, to make its weave evident—it had to look handmade, since only handmade fabrics showed a great deal of the weave. What's more, it had to look handmade even if it was actually made on a machine. If a fabric that looked hand-

New Weave

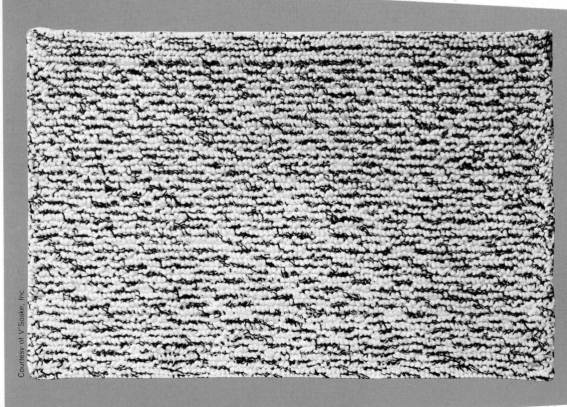

V'Soske was and continues to be a leader in the field of wool carpets. This one, from the mid-1950s, would have lent textural interest to a sparely-furnished interior.

Courtesy of V'Soske, Inc

Courtesy of the Cranbook Academy of Art Museum

Unusual colors and the metallic sheen of Lurex lend a bit of flash to this synthetic wool and cotton fabric. The handwoven upholstery was designed by Marianne Strengell in 1956.

The vivid hues of Jack Lenor Larsen's *Remoulade* fabric distinguish it from many of the woven fabrics of the fifties, which had a drabber, more repressed look.

made could be made on a power loom, so much the better. Indeed, creating such fabrics was a major concern of many handweavers at this time, and quite in keeping not only with Bauhaus tenets but with those of the influential Cranbrook Academy as well, where crafts and design were given equal emphasis. Designers such as Dorothy Liebes, Jack Lenor Larsen, Marianne Strengell, Eszter Haraszty, Evelyn Hill, and Suzanne Huegenon (the last four of whom worked for Knoll's fabric division) were all interested in developing power-loom techniques capable of producing fabrics in wool, cotton, nylon, rayon, viscose, tow linen, jute fibers, and metallic Lurex that had a hand-loomed look. At the same time handweaving continued, and several designers, like Liebes, created costly, richly textured fabrics for individual clients, while companies like V'Soske turned out sumptuous, hand-loomed carpeting and rugs.

Textile designers were not merely interested in texture for its own sake. ''Organic design'' was the rage, and though that term was subjected to myriad interpretations, according to Eliot Noyes, who in 1940 was head of MOMA's Department of Industrial Design, it basically referred to a type of design that featured ''an harmonious organization of the parts within the whole, according to structure, material and purpose.'' The exposed weave of a fabric or carpeting was viewed as honest and architectural. Its rhythms would continue, emphasize, and harmonize with those established by the structure and furniture of a space, and offset its hard edges. Texture could be used to manipulate the light in a space by reflecting it in ways that would enhance the design. These refinements were only visible to the tutored eye.

Textured fabrics and carpeting were appealing for a more practical reason, too: they hid dirt and were quite durable. This made them appealing to architects, designers, their clients, and to consumers. The range of items available included to-the-trade-only items created by the decade's leading designers and the more functional home furnishings that were easily maintained and preserved.

Pattern Play

Like texture, pattern in fabrics and wallcoverings was seen as a way of warming up the hard-edged Modern interiors of the fifties. The range of patterns available at all prices was remarkably wide. The prevailing Bauhaus influence evident in highly textured fabrics and carpeting, however, gave way to those of folk and fine art. Patterns inspired by primitive art were popular, especially when these were given the sort of humorous twist they had received in the art of Pablo Picasso, Joan Miró, Paul Klee, and Alexander Calder. (Calder actually designed wallpaper, which was manufactured and sold by Laverne.) As William J. Hennessey wrote in *Modern Furniture for the Home,* this humor was thought of as ''consistent with our informal living.''

Lighthearted though they were, these primitive-style designs carried with them a welter of connotations. Their childlike simplicity seemed a response to a civilization in the throes of a decidedly adult infatuation with a technology that—for all its promise—many found overwhelming. Even patterns that featured such contemporary imagery as television screen shapes were rendered with self-conscious imprecision, as if to say that these things need not be looked at too clearly or considered in too much detail. And then, asymmetrical and freely drawn as they were, the patterns seemed to defy the rigid conformism that dominated America in the fifties. These quirky designs offered a means by which people could humanize boxy rooms that were filled with mass-produced furniture.

These sophisticated-primitive patterns were either completely abstract or highly stylized depictions of figures or objects. Other patterns were available in the 1950s as well, offering more lifelike figures or even entire scenes. These served as conversation pieces. When used in public spaces such as restaurants, theaters, or bowling alleys, they often served to establish a theme that tied in with whatever activity took place there. Yet even these patterns display a marked off-handedness that links them to the more straightforwardly primitive fifties patterns.

Patterned fabrics and wallcoverings appealed to both the hardcore Modernists and the average American consumer. The Modernists, however, favored smaller-scaled geometric patterns, like those Alexander Girard designed for the Herman Miller Co. Like textured fabrics, these were meant to accent rather than conflict with a room's architecture. Middle America, on the other hand, favored splashier patterns for contemporary interiors. And for those with more conservative tastes, traditional florals were still available. While florals were less fashionable than abstract and primitive patterns, designers like Jack Lenor Larsen and D. D. and Leslie Tillett did create suave, stylized florals that offered a thoughtful compromise between tradition and Modernism.

The boomerang shape, omnipresent in much fifties design, graced Formica's *Skylark* plastic laminate pattern *(left)* of the mid-1950s. It took Italy's Memphis designers to revive an interest in patterned plastic laminates like this one. Thanks to them, that revival is now thriving. Formica has even expressed interest in creating some new patterns of its own.

Neon shapes that recall fifties boomerang motifs are suspended from the ceiling of New York City's popular Be Bop Café *(right)*.

Richard M. Ross

Courtesy of Greeff Fabrics

Courtesy of Greenwich Auction Gallery

In this "allegorical" fabric *(left),* Nature/Representation (the tree) and Civilization/Abstraction (the rigidly rectilinear Modern-style perspective lines) enjoy a uniquely peaceful coexistence. Fabrics like these are available at the Greenwich Auction Gallery.

This labyrinthine fifties pattern *(right)* would work well in some of today's spare interiors.

A fairly dependable way to determine where a fifties pattern fit into the scheme of things: the flatter and more geometric the design, the more "highbrow" the fabric or wallcovering. *Timber* was designed for Greeff Fabric by Angelo Testa—definitely an example of "Good Design."

Designers Inez Foose and Tom Hill have stenciled the walls in the Gümex Showroom with playful fifties-inspired patterns. This is a clever approach, given that, unlike fabric, the wallpapers of the fifties are usually not easy to come by in quantities large enough to cover whole walls.

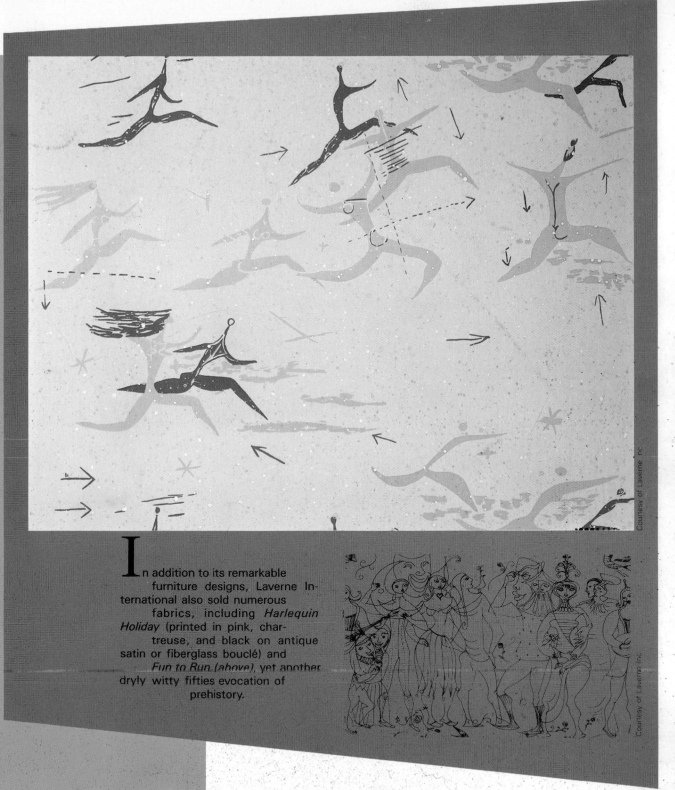

Alexander Calder's mobiles and Yves Tanguy's biomorphic forms are the direct inspirations for this brilliantly colored 1950s fabric, which most likely would have been used for draperies.

In addition to its remarkable furniture designs, Laverne International also sold numerous fabrics, including *Harlequin Holiday* (printed in pink, chartreuse, and black on antique satin or fiberglass bouclé) and *Fun to Run (above)*, yet another dryly witty fifties evocation of prehistory.

Geroge Nelson's *Ball* clock, designed for the Howard Miller Clock Company, recalls classroom models of molecules. It did not offend the tenets of fifties "Good Design," as most of the other objects shown here did.

Decorating in Extremis

Despite the stylistic differences, American furniture of the 1950s shared one common characteristic: all of it, even those pieces derived from traditional models, was almost wholly lacking in ornamentation. No carving or inlay marred sleek wood surfaces, while metal was presented in the most straightforward manner possible, without curlicues or incised designs. Patterned fabrics and wallcoverings offered only some relief from these stark forms, as did the scads of designer-created accessories, some of them functional and others purely decorative, that had a more playful quality about them.

To call them whimsical is to put it mildly. These accessories were *extreme*. A lamp base, for example, might look *extremely* abstract or primitive or scientific, or else it might hark back to some *extremely* remote period in time. The idea was to soar far beyond bland, everyday life, fueled by that exuberant postwar optimism. Indeed, expansiveness was a major theme in the American design of the decade. Americans reflected their sense of freedom through this design consciousness; they felt free to roam through time, appropriating decorative motifs from the furthest reaches of an imaginary future and a glamorized, superficially understood past. Historical or scientific accuracy was not a necessity. A decorative object merely had to have the *look* of, say, a prehistoric cave painting or a classroom model of the atom. The more extreme the look, the better—and the better it expressed the fact that fifties Americans could have anything they wanted. Nothing, no matter how far away in space or time, exceeded their grasp.

This taste for extremity is particularly obvious in many of the lamps and lighting fixtures of the period. These offered designers a chance to exercise their imaginations in a more whimsical fashion. They ranged from George Nelson's "bubble" lamps, meant to hang in clusters like mutant grapes, to Light-o-lier's zany chandelier named "Sputnik" after the Soviet satellite. The less highbrow a lamp was, the more outra-

Courtesy of El Internacional

Tim Street-Porter

What, then, *was* the consumables explosion of the fifties (echoed by the going-off-in-all-directions boomerang-on-boomerang form of this ceramic, wall-hung planter)? Comedy? Tragedy? Both? At any rate, back in the 1950s, you did not have to know that these masks stood for "The Theater."

These fascinating fifties lamps revolve in the window of El Internacional, a New York City restaurant and tapas bar created by artist Antonio Miralda and Montse Guillen.

A fleet of fifties ashtrays, each one a boomerang: These colorful pieces can perk up the rooms of smokers and non-smokers alike.

With the ascendancy of art furniture in the late 1970s and early 1980s, the Miesian credo of form follows function went right out the plate glass window. As of 1966—the year Robert Venturi's *Complexity and Contradiction in Architecture* was published—some American architects had begun working toward a design style enriched with blatant symbolism and historical allusions, a striking contrast to that in which all features of a building were pared down to their bare essentials. In fact, most of the glass-and-steel boxes

today's exaggerated free-form art furniture, while eye-catching and witty, is not always practical. This is as true of American pieces as of those designed in Italy. (By the mid-1970s, many Italian designers had already fallen under the fifties spell, and the current interest in American furniture of the 1950s among American art furniture designers and craftspeople was surely sparked by the direction Italian design had taken.) Today, both the Italians and the Americans appropriate the garish colors and outlandish forms of that

Future Perfect

of the fifties only *looked* functional and efficient and might be construed as unintentionally symbolic in their own right. But today, while function is still important to architects, freely admitted symbolism has become a major concern.

Current furniture designers have picked up on what the architects have been doing. Often they have gone beyond it. According to some young designers, it no longer matters whether a chair is comfortable or practical. Only its looks count and the statement those looks make.

In light of this new approach, it is not surprising that fifties designs—especially the more futuristic ones—have provided these designers with inspiring models. Back in the 1950s, that futuristic, free-form furniture was meant to make a splash. If it was functional, fine. If not, well—it had already made its point.

In fact, much free-form furniture of the fifties *was* fairly comfortable. But

decade and make frank use of mass-produced materials like plastic laminate in an effort to defy established standards of ''good'' and ''bad'' design. Rebelling against the sterile and—as some claim—elitist purity of Modern furniture, these designers have responded with gutsy designs. A desire to shock and a real, almost childlike delight in vivid colors and fantastic shapes have led both American and Italian designers to emulate what some consider the sleazier, cheapest-looking fifties pop designs, the kind most often described as ''so bad they're good.'' Their own pieces, however, are either one-of-a-kind or made in limited quantities for a small market, and therefore they sport expensive price tags.

Because they are so costly, these pieces are rarely used to furnish an entire home. Employed sparingly, however, they can be wonderfully amusing and can bring a note of humor to even the most serious room. But there is

Without actually quoting any particular piece of fifties furniture, Italian designer Paolo Deganello evokes the futuristic pieces of that period very vividly with his free-form ''Torso'' lounge chair *(above)*, available from Atelier International.

Along with the boomerang, the kidney shape cropped up in countless fifties designs, from cocktail tables to swimming pools. Today's art furniture designers have taken a shine to the kidney once more, as is evident in Steve Madsen's 1983 *Moving Violation* table *(right)*.

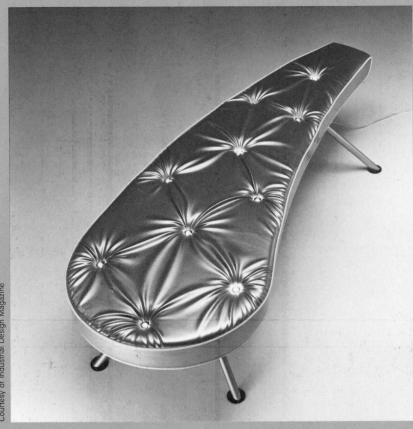

Colored lights flash from the button tufting of this fifties kidney-shaped *Crocodile* bench by Japanese designer Sinya Okayama.

also something poignant about these designs, based as they are on a style rejected for being trashy and outmoded. The classics of fifties Modern design may have been meant for the ages, but today's fifties kitsch-inspired furniture promises to date swiftly. This, of course, is the point being made by its designers who, living under the threat of nuclear holocaust, are well aware of life's fragility and the fact that nothing—not even good design—lasts forever.

Along with art furniture designers, some larger furniture manufacturers have begun to re-examine American fifties designs, though in a less playful-profound way. Reasonably priced chairs with the sort of black wrought-iron legs that during the 1950s became synonymous with Modern design are making a comeback, while some firms are reviving designs that went out of fashion twenty-five years

ago. Others offer strangely colored, asymmetrical pieces which, though unrelated to actual fifties pieces, have a funky air that ads tout, inaccurately but enticingly, as the so-called fabulous fifties. A number of fabric manufacturers are also coming out with 1950s-inspired patterns. These tend to be refined updates of the original designs, somewhat slicker, with the kind of subtle, ambiguous pastel colors that figure so prominently in the eighties design palette.

While some prefer contemporary reinterpretations of fifties pieces, others would sooner buy the real thing. Fortunately, many of the manufacturers of the original 1950s designs can still produce them today. Deemed Modern classics thirty years ago, those designs have stayed in production ever since. With the fifties revival, however, some of the more idiosyncratic designs are reappearing as well, and

these are sure to meet with warm response from those whose tastes run toward the contemporary. In some cases, a manufacturer may even be able to turn out a fifties design which, while not currently in his or her line, can still be produced should a customer place a large enough order for it.

If a 1950s original has gone out of production permanently, there is always the possibility of finding it in one of the fifties "antique" shops that have sprung up in many large American cities over the past five years. In many cases, the 1950s originals available in these nostalgia shops are actually less costly than the one-of-a-kind or limited-edition eighties updates—and, insofar as the furniture goes, are also often more comfortable. Those accustomed to the ultra-exaggerated "fabulous fifties" updates may be taken aback at how sedate these originals now look by comparison.

5

Interior Design

The Space Age

Courtesy of Knoll International

Julius Shulman

The interiors of Skidmore, Owings and Merrill's headquarters for the Connecticut General Life Insurance Company in Hartford were designed by Knoll Associates. In a pamphlet published upon the building's grand opening in 1957, the advantages of the space were noted by J.B. Wilde: "An unexpected dividend is the greater intimacy in which we spend our working day. In vertical buildings, where quick elevators take one from a small work level to the street level, there are few spontaneous meetings, few casual interchanges of work experiences. Here in the . . . lounges and on the daily routes of travel through the building we are getting to know each other better." The furniture seen here was designed by Florence Knoll.

It is curious that, amid material abundance, Americans in the fifties should have made empty space a central feature of their interior design. But by this time, architect Mies van der Rohe's aesthetic of pure, severe forms had won many American adherents, and so both newly built public edifices and private homes became veritable paeans to the void. It wasn't only the vanguard architects and designers who loved openness; even the editors of fairly conservative magazines like *House Beautiful* hymned "our wonderful 20th century concept of space . . . the free and easy movement

from the house to the garden and back to the house. . . . vistas for the eye to roam or relax in—indoors and out and upwards."

And so, in fifties interiors, walls and rooms became things of the past. Flowing space and the open plan constituted *the* look of the day. It was an especially desirable fashion for the glass-walled Modern homes so popular at the time. There, inside and outside merged in an almost uninterrupted continuum, and interior space felt as boundless as the great outdoors. Many people, even those living in city apartments, modestly scaled

suburban homes, and older houses— at least those who embraced the Modern style—favored austere emptiness over cozy clutter. They bought furniture that was light and airy and used as little of it as possible, to keep the space flowing. What furniture they had was grouped according to function. One archipelago of pieces was the living "room"; another, which included table and chairs, was the dining "room"; and that space over there, with all the cabinets and appliances, was the "kitchen." Space-consuming lamps often gave way to overhead, recessed lighting fixtures or illumi-

nated plastic panels that were at once a ceiling and a source of light. Flooring materials were continuous throughout a space, to enhance the sense of openness. Because there were no "rooms," the idea of a room's having a specific function gave way to that of multipurpose spaces, the function of which could change depending on the occasion.

Open plans proliferated in offices as well. Within a work environment, the continuum was more than a matter of appearance; open space did encourage the kind of even communications flow between workers that kept big

Julius Shulman

In the living room of the home, the classic "Good Design" of the 1950s finds itself in a spare, open space ideally suited to its sculptural forms.

Quite apart from the furniture (including pieces by Charles Eames and George Nelson), the space itself looks like it would be a pleasure to be in—that notwithstanding all the bad press today's postmodernists have given to houses with window walls instead of proper windows and "spaces" rather than clearly demarcated rooms.

The city belongs to us. At least that might be the feeling one would get standing in this fifties interior, which seems to be consubstantial with the lit grid of streets fanning out just beyond its glazed walls.

corporations operating smoothly. Yet open office space also had a certain metaphorical significance. It conveyed a feeling of unimpeded corporate growth, a growth that knew no obstacles. (Indeed, under Eisenhower, big business was having an easy enough time of it.) And it made employees feel less trapped in their working places. Yes, this was the decade of the "organization man," when strict hierarchical structures enabled upper-echelon executives to move employees around the country like pawns. Still, the offices themselves made corporations seem like healthy, rational places to be,

the sort of places whose clean lines and simple, open areas lent an idealized quality to whatever went on in them. How could anything go wrong in such crisp, orderly interiors? How could things get complicated or messy?

Modern designers emphasized functionality, but in fact there was nothing particularly functional about many of these open spaces, especially residential ones. True, in homes, less clutter meant easier cleaning. But in any temperate or cool climate, heating open-plan homes was more costly than heating those with fixed rooms.

And of course lack of privacy became a problem when there weren't any walls. These practical considerations however, were beside the point. George Nelson (who, in addition to being an innovative designer, also wrote a number of witty books on design during the 1950s) noted in *Living Spaces* that "it is not efficiency that we are looking for, but freedom from dimensional barriers."

Freedom from barriers—it was a very fifties notion. Indeed, it was not only the American government and American big business that sought to expand their power freely all over an

unresisting world. Average middle-class citizens wanted to do some expanding of their own. Russell Lynes, in *The Tastemakers*, observed a trend during the 1950s toward *outward*—as opposed to upward—mobility: that is, the desire to move from a newer, smaller house in a cramped suburb out to a bigger house in an older, more spacious suburb. That longing for continual outward movement was reflected by the open spaces of the day. And those spaces hinted at the next frontier—*outer* space—that, by the end of the decade, America would be preparing to conquer.

In his 1952 book *Living Spaces*, George Nelson joked that, given the postwar American penchant for open spaces in homes, it was likely that sooner or later there would be no rooms in houses at all and maybe no window walls, either. In fact, interior designers of the period were constantly faced with the problem of how to break up open space for privacy and storage areas without destroying the flow. They also needed to distinguish, say, the area where people socialized from the area where they slept.

The designers of the time offered many solutions to the problem. There was, for example, the free-standing storage unit. A house without walls obviously lacked closets, too. These storage units gave people places to put away their belongings. Some units featured a grid of drawers and open areas, others were solid pieces of furniture. In keeping with the Modernist aesthetic, both were completely unornamented. And just so these units wouldn't look

A House Divided

Julius Shulman

A lightweight, fiberglass curtain divides one large space into separate children's rooms.

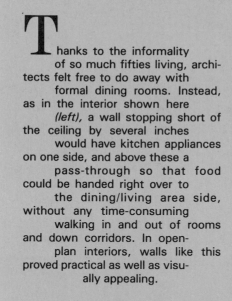

Julius Shulman

T hanks to the informality of so much fifties living, architects felt free to do away with formal dining rooms. Instead, as in the interior shown here *(left)*, a wall stopping short of the ceiling by several inches would have kitchen appliances on one side, and above these a pass-through so that food could be handed right over to the dining/living area side, without any time-consuming walking in and out of rooms and down corridors. In open-plan interiors, walls like this proved practical as well as visually appealing.

"B ooks"—so the title of an Anthony Powell novel has it—"do furnish a room." And divide one, too, as they do this one *(right)*.

Julius Shulman

too solid, they always stopped a few inches short of the ceiling; perched on 4-inch-high legs, they could stop short of the floor, too: that way, there was no mistaking them for real walls.

Screens offered another means of setting areas off from one another in an open-plan home. The imagination of a skilled designer knew no limits when it came to screens. An imaginative craftsperson might make one simply with regularly spaced strands of cord stretched taut between floor and ceiling or with strips of colorful plastic beads fused on strong nylon thread. Or the screen might be made of a lightweight, translucent material like textured fiberglass, which let light pass through while concealing whatever went on behind it (synthetic though it was, fiberglass could take on a more pleasingly natural appearance once a random scattering of real leaves and butterflies was embedded in it, as it was in some fifties screens). And then, because spare, open interiors were perceived as Modernist in spirit, *shoji* screens were also considered appropriate space dividers. Finally, bamboo folding screens and plastic accordion walls served as dividers as well, the latter proving especially useful since they could be pushed off to one side, creating more open space.

Julius Shulman

Ben Schnall

The *pièce de résistance* of many a Modern house built in the fifties was its fireplace— ideally a whole wall of native stone—in the living area. Crisply tailored yet inviting seating units would be grouped around it. The oddly reassuring effect was of doing something quite primitive (warming up around a blazing hearth) in a setting of absolute modernity.

Sticks and Stones

During the 1950s America was entering the most technologically advanced stage of its existence. Nevertheless, many of its visual artifacts betrayed a certain barbarism. We have already noted the imagery derived from primitive art featured in so many craft objects, fabrics, and accessories. And we have seen how often fifties Americans attempted to make the indoors continuous with the outdoors in their homes. With the extensive use of natural materials in interiors—especially stone and wood—these two trends

merged. The outdoors was brought inside, often in a totally unrefined state. Massive, rough-hewn stone fireplaces dominated vast, spare, Modern-style living areas like cromlechs erected by a savage tribe. In fact, the inclusion of these materials was considered a highly sophisticated gesture. Stone and wood were meant to serve as foils for the smooth, plastered surfaces and hard edges that prevailed in such a space. Indeed, those natural materials emphasized ultramodernity with a certain arrogance. Like wealthy

people who can afford to look starved, fifties Americans, with all the latest technology at their disposal, could afford to let their homes look primitive, at least in part.

But there really *was* something primitive about America at that time. Its hunger for unimpeded economic expansion was insatiable. Its consumers were encouraged to buy more and more. As the author of a 1955 article in *House Beautiful* entitled ''Too Much Is Just Right'' stated, ''Even though some may boggle at this idea

The ceilings of Modern living rooms often gave architects the chance to treat wood in a variety of interesting ways. In this interior *(left),* designed by Maral Brever, wood slats stress the horizontality of the space.

It is a look that could easily be adapted to today's living spaces, particularly lofts, although it should be noted that the effective use of this natural material is partly due to the room's rigid, clean-lined geometry. Then again, a beamed or slatted ceiling of some sort might look alright with lots of exposed pipes, too, in a space where the walls were not 100 percent perfect.

This fifties interior *(right)* was obviously inspired by the traditional domestic architecture of Japan. Indeed, there is even a tiny indoor garden beneath the room divider at the center of the space. Light for the plants would have been no problem, with that window wall.

of abundance, the truth is that man can absorb infinite amounts of betterment to his life. What we have learned about nutrition since the war proves this philosophic truth beyond the shadow of a doubt. And the truth applies to *all* areas of daily living.'' And so, like hungry lions, Americans retired to the built-in barbecue grills in their kitchens (another fifties feature) for a hearty meal of good red meat.

There was also something primitive (or, in psychological terms, regressed) about the nature of the then-new H-bomb. Of course, no interior designer or architect would have offered such theories as an explanation to a client's questions. Why was so much native stone and local wood being used in the home? Why the slate floor? Why the cork tiles? Why the walnut beams for a ceiling, why the grasscloth on the walls? As the standard rhetoric of the

day had it, these natural materials were more ''organic,'' really a relief from a technologically advanced civilization. Indeed, that blend of rough-hewn natural materials with ultrarefined geometry might be seen as a compromise between the two prevailing architectural trends of the fifties as they were embodied in the severe, rectilinear glass-and-steel buildings of Mies van der Rohe and the natural materials and exuberant curved forms that characterized much of Frank Lloyd Wright's late work (see Chapter Six, Architecture). More than anything else, though, the combination was described as fashionable and fresh, as brisk and bracing, as reminiscent of no past style within memory and therefore well-suited to the starting-out-fresh mentality of postwar America. It cropped up in stylish interiors throughout the decade.

With function a major preoccupation of fifties designers, the question of how best to organize—as opposed to how to decorate—an interior came to the fore. In residential interiors, the idea was to create order. Everything was to have its place, minimizing unsightly clutter. In open spaces, where less was definitely more, dressers and bureaus gave way to built-in storage walls that became part of a space's architecture. Built-in shelves housed books, records, and phonographs, and provided surfaces on which to display

fetched as it sounds. Indeed, in 1951 one *House Beautiful* writer went so far as to stress that now, ''for the first time in history the home can be run as systematically as a business is run.''

Still, the *real* models of efficiency were the offices of the 1950s. As Lois Wagner wrote in a 1955 issue of *Interiors,* ''Although the chairman of the board or the president of the firm may still prefer to rest his dictaphone on a Georgian bulwark, the outward sign of the progressive organization today...is crisply modern furnishings

Julius Shulman

Models of Efficiency

decorative or craft objects, while sleeping areas might include built-in headboards that had ample storage space within. (Many mass-produced ''suites'' of bedroom furniture had beds with storage headboards as well.) Some homes had ''integrated'' built-in units that included storage cabinets, drawers, a desk, and a makeup/ dressing table.

It was the kitchen, though, that inspired the greatest feats of organization—an innovation housewives welcomed in that servantless age. Just as working life could be more strictly ordered thanks to corporate structures, so housework could be controlled thanks to ''precision planning,'' with kitchens graced by color-coded cabinets, push-button ovens that turned themselves on and off, sleek plastic laminate countertops, and clearly demarcated work centers for food preparation, food storage, cooking, serving, and cleaning up. The comparison to business is not as far

from the v.p.'s on down the line. The looks of the furniture,'' she continued, ''suggests seas of alert workers zealously demonstrating previously unrealized efficiency.'' Before the fifties, there had been no systematic approach to office design. Now, however, corporate and aesthetic ways of thinking had converged to the point where both agreed that the more organized a working space was, the better.

The guiding light in fifties office design was Florence Knoll. A multitalented and phenomenally energetic woman, Knoll not only designed furniture and ran her own successful furniture company, but she also headed the Knoll Planning Unit, which created interiors for a number of important corporate headquarters in the 1950s. These *were* models of efficiency. Storage problems were studied closely, and solutions that were both workable and good-looking were offered. Desks and storage modules were designed to make the work routines of both execu-

Julius Shulman

Fifties built-ins, efficient though they were, could also have an air of sleek glamour about them. This interior, which could perhaps be mistaken for eighties design, is a case in point.

Fifties Americans loved television. In this living room, television is given its own built-in compartment. When in use, a door is slid shut, and the set is hidden by a booth wall surface. The built-in look, the epitome of 1950s modernity, was in fact often used to mask the more technological aspects of the modern world. Even today, interior designers like to keep the television out of sight until its services are called for.

Julius Shulman

This fifties kitchen looks dazzlingly modern. Yet there were drawbacks to setups like these that did not go undetected by critical theorist Theodor W. Adorno, who emigrated from Nazi Germany to the United States. In *Minima Moralia*, Adorno took a dim but highly original view of such models of efficiency: "Not least to blame for the withering of experience," he wrote, "is the fact that things, under the law of pure functionality, assume a form that limits contact with them to mere operation, and tolerates no surplus, either in freedom of conduct or in autonomy of things, which would survive as the core of experience, because it is not consumed by the moment of action."

tives and secretaries as uncomplicated as possible. What's more, the design helped to define tasks as well as to define the corporate structure, with offices literally furniture- and color-coded to indicate the rank of their occupants. Ornamentation, of course, was banned. Walls stayed blank. And despite bright colors and a concerted effort to make working spaces lively and conducive to productivity, the overall effect was one of the strictest uniformity.

It was not that variety was missing. But these reductivist interiors, where even the slightest contrast of textures was meant to be perceived—and to be aesthetically pleasing—could be fully appreciated only by those initiated into the Modernist sensibility. A Modernist would have been thrilled with the transition from, say, white vinyl tiles in one work area to asphalt tiles in an adjacent one (to name two widely used flooring materials of the 1950s). To the less sensitized observer, it would simply have been a question of going from one ordinary sort of floor tile to another, certainly nothing to get excited about. It was like having someone accustomed to Broadway show tunes sit down and listen to a Webern quartet, provoking the inevitable question, "Where's the melody?" For Webern, beauty resided in the transition from interval to interval, from tone to tone. For the Modernist designers, beauty resided in the transition from one material to the next. To the uninitiated, it failed to make a lot of sense.

It was in these extremely efficient interiors that the conformist spirit that gripped fifties America was expressed most vividly, if unintentionally. The Modernist designers who created them had thought of themselves as rebels sweeping away all past notions of interior design. In fact, their devotion to absolute order fitted in almost too neatly with the aims of corporations at the time. Fabric designer Jack Lenor Larsen summed it up nicely when he recalled, in a 1982 issue of *Industrial Design*, that "the establishment took up modern architecture and design. The designers got too busy to be revolutionaries. We thought we'd won, but we were also bought off."

If fifties Americans craved efficient interiors, they had not forgotten the old saw about all work and no play making Johnny a dull boy. At the same time that Modern designers pared down, built in, and organized space, other designers were exercising their flair for fantasy. Like many of the decorative accessories of the 1950s, these fantasy interiors often had an extreme quality about them. Again, both the remote past and faraway future were evoked—particularly with murals, which were very popular during this period. And again, there was that same unconcern with historical accuracy. Historical motifs were appropriated and then simplified to lend them a more contemporary look; everyone agreed that technology had made life simpler and more convenient, and it seemed sensible to extend that simplicity to decorative imagery as well. As these motifs were being simplified, they were also being flattened, so their exotic air had a blandness and a hard-to-define lack of sensuality. This is perhaps one of the most difficult things to

Fantastic!

The baroque *Chez Bon Bon* in the Fontainebleau Hotel in Miami Beach, designed by Morris Lapidus, verges on the surreal. The architect exaggerated and/or cross-bred traditional ornamental motifs and invented some all his own. Everything looks slightly over-scaled, which only adds to the appeal. If the Modern rooms of the fifties seemed to foster circumspection in their occupants, this room would encourage the most unbridled self-indulgences. It is only a matter of time before younger American architects begin reassessing Lapidus's brilliantly imaginative work.

Courtesy of estate of Bruce Goff

This rendering of an interior for the residence of Dr. and Mrs. Emil Gutman, designed by Bruce Goff, gives some idea of the startling originality of this architect's work. In color, rooms like this one, which Goff designed in the mid-fifties, are even more astounding, although their seemingly haphazard (and who knows, maybe they *are* haphazard—so what?) welter of glimmering surfaces, natural materials, and richly worked fabrics are difficult to capture in photographs.

Courtesy of Morris Lapidus Assoc.

convey about much fifties design: that is, how even at its most flamboyant, it also looked rather plain, as if the fantasy never went far enough.

Fantastic touches often lent character to otherwise undistinguished residential interiors. To give readers ideas for perking up lifeless rooms, the decorating magazines periodically ran photographs of interiors with supposedly clever, exotic looks. For instance, there was *House & Garden*'s ''Harlequin'' look of 1954, possibly a takeoff on harlequin sunglasses (and certainly a reprocessing of the harlequin imagery that figured in the cubist paintings of Braque and Picasso). The walls boasted a geometric diamond motif, and the accessories were ''practically audible,'' the point being to ''bring excitement to the room.'' A popular look in wallpaper murals involved ancient Rome, stylized versions of triumphal arches and centurions that cast long shadows while, behind them, converging perspective lines evoked the infinity of distance—influenced by Giorgio de Chirico. And then, of course, there was the primitive look so dear to the decade's designers, that made life in caves and grass huts seem as effortless as life had become in new 1950s homes.

Today, these gimmicks look awfully tacky, taking the most superficial features of fine art while ignoring its deeper significance. A Braque or a de Chirico makes sense if it is seen as the expression of someone's imagination; but the minute the images of these artists are commercialized (as they were in fifties fantasy interiors) and divested of that psychological significance, they become banal symbols which stand for little more than Fine Art, capital F capital A—that is, fine art deprived of all content. However, it is this very lack of content that makes these images so fascinating; the superficiality makes them so haunting, suggesting something (but what?) lurking just beneath the surface.

Not all fifties fantasy interiors were this superficial. The Oklahoma architect Bruce Goff, for example, working far from mainstream American Modernism in terms of both outlook and geography, was endowed with a vivid

Robert Harber's 1980 painting *Neptune Lounge* depicts a bar in which a small aquarium sheds light even as it provides drinkers with something to look at apart from one another. Its matter-of-fact weirdness recalls many a 1950s cocktail lounge. Others may be reminded of the unusual displays that figure in the works of the French writer Raymond Roussel.

imagination that enabled him to create rooms unlike anything else being done at the time. His highly idiosyncratic style seemed to be a cross between art nouveau and set design from fifties science fiction movies. Luxurious, gaudy materials as well as natural materials were employed extensively, in a refreshing about-face from the restrained Modern interiors of the day. The Lavernes, too, although known primarily for their furniture, created murals that, with their biomorphic, cosmic imagery, lent interiors far less elaborate than those Goff designed an otherworldly air. The Lavernes also manufactured wallcovering murals, some featuring colorful marbleized patterns, others with blowups of the dizzying architectural fantasias of Piranesi. These, too, endowed a space with an aura of mystery that Modern design lacked. Finally, there were the unbelievably extravagant public interiors of the Miami Beach hotels designed by architect Morris Lapidus. Lapidus grabbed historical motifs and ideas from all over the place and made up quite a few of his own, including a huge terrarium shaped like a diamond. These he put together in one big, splendid package, to assure guests that they were most definitely on vacation from the real world. As Lapidus himself put it, "We've let man's primitive desire for decoration come out—and brought it up to his contemporary level. . . . I've given these people something to gape at. You might call it a tasteful three-ring circus."

Courtesy of Morris Lapidus Assoc.

This may look like a still from a movie—from the dream sequence of a movie, perhaps—but in fact the people and the bar (the latter designed by Morris Lapidus) are real.

Courtesy of Herman Miller, Inc.

Courtesy of El Internacional

Living Color

As we have seen in the previous chapter, people's taste in furniture during the 1950s ran from the Modern to what might be called neoconservative. There were also plenty of Americans who still preferred to live with reproductions (usually far from faithful ones) of colonial pieces or oriental pieces or French provincial pieces. But no matter if one favored contemporary or traditional furniture, insofar as color went, one's allegiance was solely to the present. "Gone is the day of worrying whether a color is 'correct for the style of my furniture,'" wrote a *House*

Beautiful editor in 1951. "Americans are learning to forget rules about color. They are learning to use their own eyes." Indeed, in the decade when America came into its own, its citizens went mad for bright, bold colors, using whichever ones they pleased in every room they lived in.

Sometimes these colors might be employed only as discreet accents—a few flat throw pillows on a sofa, say, or a cocktail table with a mosaic top or draperies or even an entire wall—in interiors where earth tones and beiges dominated. Designer Donald Deskey

even came out with a line of splotchily colored furniture (anomalous even in the fifties) made of cast aluminum and polychrome Micarta. In tones ranging from blue-into-violet to red-into-sienna, they provided some of the color accents thought to be so appropriate for the more sophisticated spaces of the fifties.

But the further away from high style one got, the more outrageous the colors became. As one *House & Garden* editor informed readers in 1954, "Color creates a prettier world everywhere you turn. . . . If you choose, you

can cook in a pink kitchen, sleep between candy-striped sheets. . . . You can put pink and orange side by side, mix blue with green, team lilac with red . . . ." A cautious use of matching colors was considered adequate, but lots of colors in previously unheard-of combinations was far more desirable.

In one sense, color was used sparingly. A room might boast only four hues—say turquoise, beige, dark brown, and cherry red. These, however, would be applied in big slabs: a slab here for the sofa; two slabs for those walls, another slab for the floor

In keeping with the antidecoration stance adopted by most Modernist designers and architects, the trend insofar as color went was to use it not decoratively but architecturally. Color defined the various planes of a space. That was why colors were not meant to blend in with one another and why subtle, indefinite hues were avoided. The idea was for each surface to stand out in high, sharp relief.

Colors made fifties interiors literally hum with energy. It was an optimistic time and an exuberant use of color—in cars, clothing, graphics, and interiors—offered one more way of expressing that optimism. Even some of the bomb shelters of the period were colorful. (In *The Glory and the Dream*, William Manchester describes one in Los Angeles with "brightly painted concrete walls [and] shamrock green plastic carpeting.") But if these colors had something up-to-date about them, there was—as is the case with so much fifties design—something primitive, or at least folkloric about them, too. At that time, many designers took an interest in the primitive and folk art of Mexico, and indeed part of the 1950s palette was borrowed from that country's contemporary fabrics and art and the feathered robes worn in its Aztec past.

As has been suggested previously, primitivist fifties design can be seen as a reflection—perhaps even a glorification—of the savage quality of fifties capitalism and military prowess. But there is another way to interpret it: that is, as an indication of a society growing more and more aware of the rich variety of foreign cultures. Higher education and television both served to broaden people's knowledge of the world during the fifties. In turn, many people seemed to grow more curious about the world around them. Material pleasures were pursued with gusto, but so was knowledge. And so one might say that just as Americans opened themselves up to the spectrum of foreign cultures, so in their homes they were now willing to experiment with a broad spectrum of colors. Isolationism and muted tones may have prevailed before World War II. In the colorful postwar years, America was ready to look around at the rest of the world.

I Internacional *(left),* the New York City tapas bar and restaurant, has recreated a fifties en‑ ment. It boasts a curvy, glittery g—a dazzling eighties update of es interior architectural trait.

In the interior of a late 1950s showroom for the Herman Miller Company *(far left),* planes of color have been used architecturally to define the space. The persimmon *Marshmallow* sofa, designed in 1956 by George Nelson Associates, is more than a mere color accent; it has an architectural presence as well.

Well-known for his interiors at Radio City Music Hall, Donald Deskey also designed numerous pieces of furniture in several styles, ranging from art deco in the late 1920s to this uncategorizable fifties-style chest of drawers, part of a 1959 collection for Charak. It might be seen as predecessor of the colorful, plastic laminate-covered furniture Italy's Memphis designers are creating today.

Beyond Good and Bad

Langdon Clay. Courtesy of the designer Vincas Meilus

George Ross

This interior, in architect Vincas Meilus's own loft, is character-ized by the asymmetrical quadrilaterals seen in the graphics and roadside signs of the 1950s.

The interior design of the 1950s in-spires a range of American designers today, from those working well within the mainstream to those in the van-guard. More conservative designers limit themselves to a few of the best-known fifties pieces—an Eames molded plywood chair or Saarinen's pedestal table—deploying them in sleek minimalist environments where their sculptural quality stands out viv-idly against spare, monochromatic backgrounds. In many instances, be-cause this furniture has never gone out of production, it does not necessarily read as "fifties" but simply as classic Modern design. As such it connotes not a nostalgic yearning for the past but fashionable good taste.

On the other hand, an increasing number of collectors snap up original 1950s furniture, much of it no longer available from its manufacturers, and they design their own settings for these treasured finds. Some group American pieces together with fifties Scandinavian and Italian furniture and accessories in interiors that are hard-edged and neutral; although these do not evoke actual fifties rooms, they let the designs speak for themselves. Other collectors strive for a total 1950s look, with fabrics and colors derived from the rooms of that decade. Most collectors find fifties pieces to be as sturdy as any new piece of furniture they might buy, quite apart from the visual beauty. Their lightness and func-tionality are as welcome today as the were thirty years ago. Many of th open pieces from the 1950s are co sidered ideal for today's increasing cramped living quarters.

Today's most adventurous desig ers use 1950s furniture—particular the wildly futuristic free-form pieces as a jumping-off point for extravaga designs of their own. They take

Courtesy of Hadler-Rodriguez Gallery

The wall of this Manhattan loft, painted by Philip Maberry—an artist known for his ceramics and fabrics—with his associate Scott Walker, is a takeoff on the native stone walls that graced the living rooms of so many Modern houses of the fifties. The cartoon colors of these "rocks," however, are strictly eighties.

Working with designer Bob Crabtree, Malcolm Kelso, an avid collector of 1950s designs, created this thoroughly up-to-the-minute living room. Here, fifties pieces—including a cocktail table by Paul McCobb—take on contemporary sleekness when set against bleached floors and pristine walls. Fifties icon Marilyn Monroe puts in an appearance as an airbrushed blowup on foam card.

A pair of the molded and bent birch plywood dining chairs that Charles Eames and Ray Kaiser Eames designed in 1946—and that were seen in stylish Modern interiors throughout the 1950s—grace a contemporary space designed by Patino/Wolf Associates. The chair's strong, sculptural form makes it well-suited to minimalist rooms like this one, which is far more austere than the equally spare but warmer-toned Modern rooms of the fifties.

Peter Vitale. Design by Patino/Wolf Associates, Inc.

furniture and create settings around it that are far more idiosyncratic and "fabulous" than anything ever done during the supposedly "fabulous fifties." Alive to the humor and exuberance of these pieces, they place them in rooms that are so outrageously high energy in their screaming hues, amoeboid shapes, and clashing patterns as to seem like parodies, bizarre mutations of a style that was extreme to begin with. Yet the parodies are almost always affectionate. By exaggerating "vulgar" fifties motifs, these interior designers, like many fifties-inspired furniture designers, poke fun at the naive optimism of a nation infatuated with new consumer goods and the advanced technology that made them possible—an optimism blind to the economic and ecological drawbacks rampant consumerism and unregulated technology would bring in their wake. At the same time, though, these designers share the sense of playfulness that was part of the fifties style.

These interior designers—they are really more artists than decorators—eschew terms like "good" and "bad" taste, preferring to join in the spirit of a mass culture that favors quantity and flash over quality and substance. No doubt people such as pop artists Roy Lichtenstein and Andy Warhol (one-time exemplar of fifties-style graphic design himself), and architects Robert Venturi, Denise Scott Brown, and Steven Izenour with their book *Learning from Las Vegas* provided the inspiration here. But a New Wave sensibility—the paradox of joyous pessimism—comes into play as well, carrying the work of these aesthetic forebears to new and daring extremes. The negative aspect of this sensibility arises out of a glorification of—and more or less uncritical acceptance of—surface flash, blatant commercialism, and the visual overkill that characterizes America today, from its suburban strips to its urban centers. And yet optimism is evident, too, in the determination to make the best of what might be easily dismissed as so much trash and the willingness to see that trash as an expression of the human spirit no less valid than more conventionally "beautiful" artifacts.

Alan Hess

6

Architecture

If fifties American and émigré architects had a patron, it was big business. Burgeoning corporations needed gleaming new headquarters that would attest to their modernity and power, and there were plenty of architects around to help provide what even by the late 1950s was termed a "corporate image."

But Frank Lloyd Wright was not one of those architects. Already an old man when the decade began, Wright had a long history of antipathy toward capitalists. His ideal clients—at least

Style, as it had been called in architecture since the early thirties—had attracted enough adherents to give Wright a run for his money. The International Style's originators—the Bauhaus architects and designers—had admired Wright's work in the 1920s and continued to respect him once they set up shop in America. But Wright detested them and their work, especially since it came to symbolize the corporate bureaucratic interests of the day. Given to showmanship, he made the most of this conflict, portray-

Wright-Minded

for his public buildings—were men who, aside from being millionaires, were more or less like himself. Rugged individualists, they were open-minded enough to let this individualist architect par excellence give them the building he pleased, and imaginative enough to grasp just what Wright was giving them. And so it is not surprising that, during the fifties, none of Wright's major buildings resulted from corporate commissions. Certainly it is hard to envision his increasingly unpredictable structures being considered as acceptable for, say, the headquarters of an insurance company (though in 1956 Wright did exceed the Modernists with his proposition for a skyscraper that was to boast 528 floors and soar a mile up into the air—a project that never was built).

Big business was not Wright's only enemy. Although by now many acknowledged him as the greatest American architect who had ever lived, Modernism—or the International

ing himself as the Last Individualist struggling heroically against the encroaching forces of conformism. Showmanship notwithstanding, Wright's late work was not nearly as influential as that of Mies van der Rohe and his followers, and the buildings Wright designed in the 1950s—many of them undisputed if eccentric masterpieces—were seen as dazzling anomalies, in no way characteristic of the decade's architecture.

Manfredo Tafuri and Francesco del Co, in their book *Modern Architecture*, argue that Wright opposed the big-business mentality and the form-follows-function formula of the Modernists. In the spirit of American transcendentalism, Wright had developed an organic approach to architecture in which a building's forms were derived from those of nature and meant to harmonize with it. Curves, and not right angles, came to play a major (though not exclusive) role in his late work. But with these

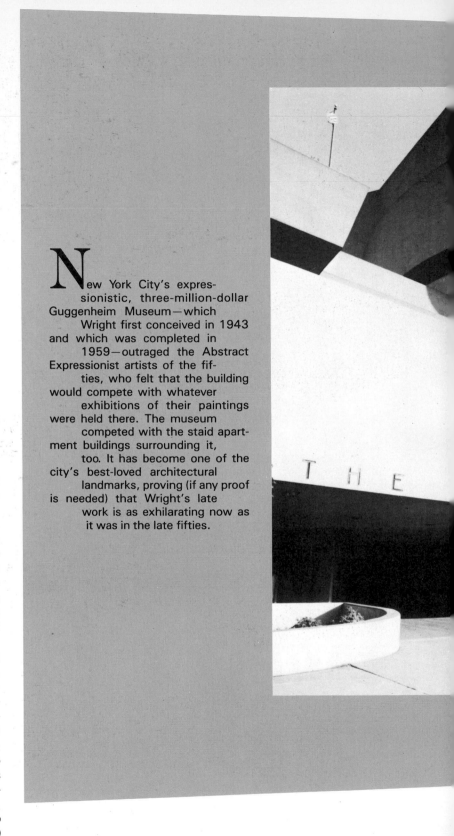

New York City's expressionistic, three-million-dollar Guggenheim Museum—which Wright first conceived in 1943 and which was completed in 1959—outraged the Abstract Expressionist artists of the fifties, who felt that the building would compete with whatever exhibitions of their paintings were held there. The museum competed with the staid apartment buildings surrounding it, too. It has become one of the city's best-loved architectural landmarks, proving (if any proof is needed) that Wright's late work is as exhilarating now as it was in the late fifties.

Built between 1953 and 1955 in Bartlesville, Oklahoma, Frank Lloyd Wright's prismatic Price Tower features angular geometries no less exuberant than the Guggenheim's soaring curves. The building boasts ornamental, stamped copper spandrels that would have been viewed with disdain by Modernist architects of the fifties.

But the Price Tower's structure—cantilevered steel embedded in concrete—was as technologically advanced as any of the structures those architects employed in their own buildings.

curves, which grew more and more outrageous during the fifties, Wright was doing more than evoking nature. There was something defiantly antifunctional about them. At times they were downright impractical, as in the Solomon R. Guggenheim Museum in New York City, whose famous spiral ramp, while successfully capturing what Wright himself called ''the atmosphere of the quiet unbroken wave,'' obliged viewers to look at the artworks displayed along it while standing on a slant. Or else Wright's forms resolutely ignored their natural surroundings, as in the Marin County Civic Center in San Rafael, California, which sits like a flying saucer fresh from Mars amid peaceful rolling hills.

According to Tafuri and del Co, these gratuitous forms bespoke a liberation from the contingencies of workaday capitalist life. But if Wright saw himself as standing in opposition to midcentury American capitalism, he assumed that stance not with bitter disenchantment but with a Nietzschean sense of ''lighthearted alienation.'' Modernist architects claimed to have cornered the market on Truth with their form-follows-function imperative, their abhorrence of chaos, and their absolute faith in technology as an end in itself. But Wright, in the fifties, was blithely telling America that there *was* no Truth, that a building could be whatever he pleased, no matter how fantastic, and technology was to be used only as a means toward that end.

It would not be wholly correct to say that Wright's fifties buildings had no effect on American architecture. Alan Gowans, in *Images of American Living*, declares that Wright's style was ''always too personal for mass emulation.'' And yet that style was most influential on the commercial roadside architecture that arose during the fifties, with its swooping, extravagant, attention-getting forms. Wright's individualism may have had an elitist cast; his unpredictable forms may have seemed private to the point of self-indulgence. But when it came time for the people to build buildings for the people, it was Wright's late work, and not Modernist glass boxes, that provided the inspiration.

Boxed In

Hedrich Blessing

Of all the former members of the Bauhaus faculty who emigrated to the United States from Nazi Germany, it was Ludwig Mies van der Rohe whose influence on American architects and designers was most profound. It is not hard to fathom the warm welcome with which many American architects greeted Mies. He was as much a visionary as Wright was, although the vision itself could not have been more different. Through his buildings, Mies sought to embrace the Industrial Age, not ignore its existence. His preferred materials, glass and steel, were industrial; his famous maxim "form follows function" was more applicable, perhaps, to an assembly-line machine than to a building. The spare, unorna-

mented, functional appearance of American factories had fascinated Mies and other Bauhaus architects back in the 1920s. A factory had to *work*, not look pretty or heroic, and so it made no difference if its structure was exposed. In time, the exposed structure was to become a Bauhaus trademark. Modernists would expose the structure of whatever they designed, whether it was a textile, a chair, or a house, out of a sense of what they called honesty.

But the architecture Mies hoped to create, while it would feature exposed structures and a factorylike simplicity of form, was not to be purely utilitarian. To Mies, simple, geometric structures were not merely functional. They

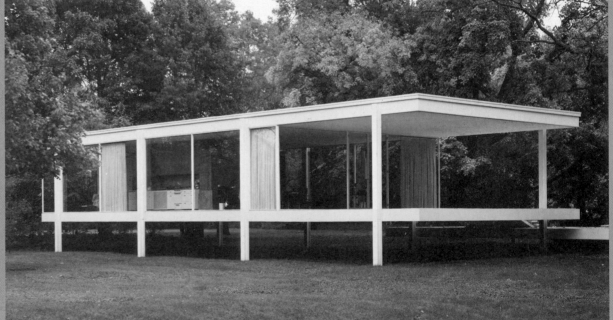

Hedrich Blessing

Mies van der Rohe's Farnsworth House, built in Fox River, Illinois between 1949 and 1959, is simply a pair of horizontal slabs floating from eight welded I-beams. As critic Charles Jencks notes, "The allusions which it makes to the Platonic world of eternal values are not quickly ridiculed by obvious shortcomings." Mies remains a controversial figure to this day.

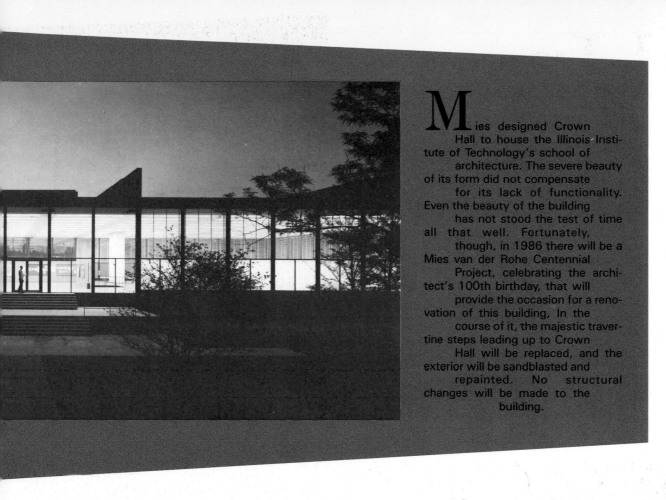

Mies designed Crown Hall to house the Illinois Institute of Technology's school of architecture. The severe beauty of its form did not compensate for its lack of functionality. Even the beauty of the building has not stood the test of time all that well. Fortunately, though, in 1986 there will be a Mies van der Rohe Centennial Project, celebrating the architect's 100th birthday, that will provide the occasion for a renovation of this building. In the course of it, the majestic travertine steps leading up to Crown Hall will be replaced, and the exterior will be sandblasted and repainted. No structural changes will be made to the building.

lso evoked a realm of *pure* forms, a timeless realm far superior to the incoherent mess of the workaday world.

It is this double intention—the desire to accept the world as it is and the desire to exceed it—that made Mies's buildings seem like the last word in modernity: utterly sleek and positive, and at the same time tragic in their yearning for an absolute, impossible purity—something that could never be. Yet there is an eerie aspect to his buildings, frozen as they are into crystalline perfection. For if, as Mies believed, less is more, then nothing—the nothing of nonbeing—is best of all. In this aspect of Mies's work, one senses a deep condescension toward the messier aspects of life. Acknowledging this condescension helps one under-

stand why, when his Seagram Building was completed, he asked that the two fountains in the plaza in front of the building be filled to the brim; that way, no one would sit on their edges and thereby destroy the perfect, inhuman symmetry of his plaza.

The philosophical underpinnings of Mies's architecture had little to do with its assimilation by corporate America. Chairmen of the board could not have cared less about idealized Platonic forms. Rather, it was the immaculate, well-ordered, up-to-the-minute *look* of these geometric buildings that must have struck corporate bigwigs as a fitting metaphor for the well-ordered bureaucracies over which they presided. And it is only understandable that they were so receptive to the ideas

of a man who could make the following statement without irony: ''The individual is losing significance . . . his destiny is no longer what interests us. The decisive achievements in all fields are impersonal, and their authors are for the most part obscure. They are part of the trend of our time toward 'anonymity' '' (quoted by Marty Jezer in *The Dark Ages: Life in the United States 1945–1960*). The ''apotheosis of the compulsive, bureaucratic spirit'' is what Charles Jencks called Miesian architecture in *Modern Movements in Architecture,* and if the bureaucracy itself did not see things that way, there was no doubt that by the end of the 1950s, when Mies's glass-and-steel boxes had spawned countless imitations in every large American city, peo-

ple viewed this kind of architecture as *the* symbol of corporate power.

In fact, Mies designed for a variety of clients in the United States during the fifties. These included the Seagram Corporation, whose New York headquarters set a precedent for that city's commercial architecture; the Illinois Institute of Technology, for which he designed a chapel and Crown Hall, its school of architecture, among other buildings; the developers of the Chicago apartment complex 860–880 Lake Shore Drive; and several private individuals, a commission from one of whom resulted in the famous Farnsworth House in Fox River, Illinois, whose owner, finding the house too impractical and costly to live in, sued Mies (and lost). All these buildings featured an extensive use of glass and steel; all benefited from the high quality of American steel craftsmanship; all conveyed a factorylike impersonality. But in his quest for absolute purity, Mies endowed his buildings with neoclassically symmetrical proportions and plans that made them seem like secular, modern-day temples even when what went on inside them was something as mundane as, say, running a large liquor company.

Mies's buildings inspired far more imitations than Wright's did during the fifties (the Miesian interiors also influenced many interior designers at the time, especially in the emphasis on open, flowing spaces). Although the originals were usually not inexpensive to build, numerous other architects managed to copy them while cutting costs considerably. Indeed, the whole notion of buildings made entirely of simple, repeated forms proved enchanting to real estate investors with their eye fixed firmly on the bottom line. Such buildings—using readily available prefabricated materials— could be built quickly and more cheaply than ones with extensive ornamentation. What's more, those buildings looked as neat and tidy as everyone hoped American life would be, now that World War II was over and the economy booming. And so, over the course of the decade, Miesian boxes arose everywhere—minus the Miesian metaphysics.

Throughout the 1950s, the infatuation on the part of American architects with the Miesian aesthetic escalated to mind-boggling proportions. Impassioned as they were, it was not long before these architects had big corporations and well-heeled private clients clamoring for pure, glass-and-steel boxes of their own.

The leader in this field was the architectural firm of Skidmore, Owings and Merrill, familiarly known as SOM. SOM took the Miesian adoration of impersonality very much to heart: not

of the utmost sophistication. People marveled at the way these mammoth yet seemingly weightless glass-and-steel slabs actually stood up. But as critic Charles Jencks wrote of Harrison and Abramovitz's Alcoa Building in Pittsburgh, Pennsylvania, after the initial sense of awe ''one has the feeling of being in the Grand Canyon or Wall Street where vast impersonal forces of economy and exploitation have taken over.''

Such was the Bauhaus legacy to America in the fifties. Some of its origi-

The Mieslings

only did it design buildings that *looked* impersonal, but the buildings themselves were usually designed in the most impersonal, anti-individualistic manner possible—that is, by committee or ''team'' that had little if any direct contact with the client. SOM's 1952 Lever House in New York, though nominally designed by Gordon Bunshaft, was—and still is—not really an exception, since it bore no trace of an individual architectural signature. The first of many glass-and-steel boxes, Lever House was, according to architectural historian John Jacobus, ''simultaneously distinctive and anonymous.'' Its glazed vertical slab of an office tower appears quite functional. Yet it is a far cry from the factories beloved by Bauhaus architects.

And so both SOM and the equally successful architectural firm of Harrison and Abramovitz turned out numerous boxes, all with the same gleaming new air about them. In all cases, the technology behind the buildings was

nal members, however, took a somewhat different approach (with the exception of Mies, who originated that look of impersonality). Walter Gropius (1883–1969), for example, in working with a group of younger American architects known as the Architects' Collaborative, designed buildings like the Harvard Graduate Center that were as rigidly rectilinear as SOM's but which lacked their gleaming, glamorous quality. The fifties buildings of Marcel Breuer, especially his private houses, were more appealing. Breuer warmed up the Bauhaus glass-and-steel look by introducing passages of wood and fieldstone on the facades of these houses, as well as by using brightly painted areas of vermilion, yellow, and ultramarine.

Other American architects of the decade provided their own variations on the Miesian formula. Philip Johnson's famous Glass House in New Canaan, Connecticut, for instance, owed much to Mies's own houses (indeed,

Marcel Breuer designed the Gagarin House in Litchfield, Connecticut, in association with Herbert Beckhard during a period between 1954 and 1955.

Philip Johnson's *Glass House* is a far cry from the work this late convert to Postmodernism is now producing. At the time it was built, the house was the last word in architectural Modernism, and Johnson made no secret of the fact that he considered Mies van der Rohe to be the greatest architect in the world.

Johnson had collaborated with Mies on the Seagram Building), but also incorporated myriad allusions to past architectural styles, not in its ornamentation (there *was* no ornamentation) but in its plan. Johnson even went so far as to publish a list of these allusions, just so people did not miss them (''people'' meaning other architects and assorted intellectuals). Designers Charles and Ray Eames, in their own Santa Monica, California, home, handled the Miesian vocabulary in a less academic manner. Their house was built entirely of factory-made, prefabricated parts. While it featured the same open, flowing expanses that Johnson's house did, the Eameses' house betrayed a keener sensitivity to materials and a more sensual manipulation of light and shadow. Craig Ellwood, another California architect, also designed several houses that resembled Mies's in their reliance on exposed

steel structures: he exhibited a far greater sensitivity to the buildings' natural surroundings, though. And then there was the designer-architect Eero Saarinen. Before shifting gears for his late, exuberant phase, Saarinen designed the General Motors Technical Center in Warren, Michigan, a restrained, boxy structure with subtle detailing that brings Mies to mind. Already, however, Saarinen was hinting at what was to come when he said that these buildings were not merely idealized forms but actually examples of ''the precise, well-made look which is the proud characteristic of industrial America'' (quoted by John Jacobus in *Twentieth-Century Architecture, The Middle Years (1940–1965)*.

If any architect seemed to be taking a decisive step forward and away from the Miesian aesthetic during the 1950s, it was Louis Kahn. Kahn still favored Miesian rectilinear forms; how-

ever, his own buildings used not only sleek glass and steel but more tactile stone and brick as well, and had a weighty, less standardized appearance that distinguished them from the usual glass-and-steel slabs.

As absolutist as Mies's formulations sounded, they did admit variations and modifications, but these were strictly for the connoisseur. To someone who knew little about architecture and could not differentiate between the subtleties of this or that approach, these Mies-inspired buildings formed a repetitious series of big, dull, anonymous boxes that looked the same wherever they were built, regardless of local character. By the mid-fifties, there were even a few architects who started seeing things that way. It was for those architects to design buildings that had personality to them—and that a wide public could enjoy.

Toward the end of *From Bauhaus to Our House*, Tom Wolfe offers an intriguing observation in regard to postwar American architecture: "For any architect to have explored an avenue such as a new, straightforward (non-ironic), exuberant (non-camp) system of decoration...would have been a revolutionary development." Earlier on, however, Wolfe suggests that such a development had already taken place—and had been essentially ignored—during the 1950s. Referring specifically to the buildings of Wright,

all too well. On the other hand, business was booming, and many Americans were having great fun buying things, going places, and enjoying the materialistic things of life with a gusto reflected vividly in the work of the above-mentioned architects, as well as in that of their lesser known California contemporary, John Lautner.

Inspired, in part, by Wright, these architects employed flamboyant forms and decoration in their buildings. This was most astonishing in the later work of Saarinen and Stone, both of whom

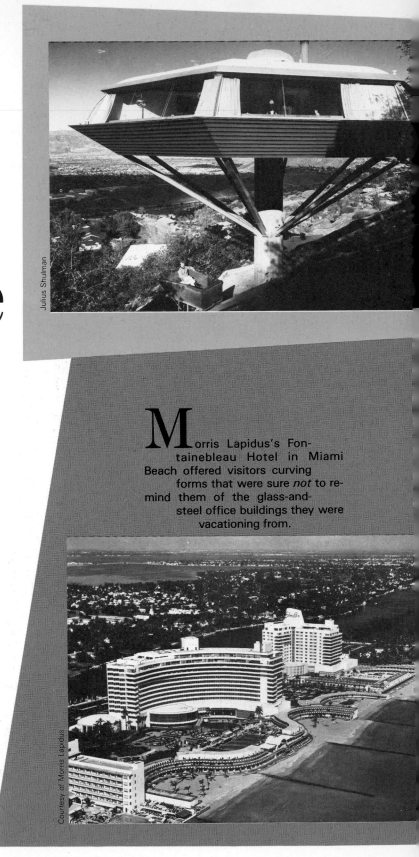

Julius Shulman

Exuberance

Saarinen, Edward Durrell Stone, Morris Lapidus, and Bruce Goff, he notes that "somehow they actually catered to the hog-stomping Baroque exuberance of American civilization." According to Wolfe, the work these architects did during the fifties was not taken seriously by the trend-setting disciples of Mies. At best, their outrageously imaginative, gaudy buildings were taken—or mistaken—for camp, something along the lines of a Busby Berkeley extravaganza. At worst, they were viewed as unspeakably vulgar, and summarily dismissed.

It would not be totally accurate to say that, dismissed or not, the buildings these men designed expressed the healthy capitalist civilization of fifties America. Fifties America *was* exuberant and sure of itself, but it was also conformist, sexually repressed, and, with the Soviet Union developing hydrogen bombs, not a little scared. And so Wolfe's argument that the Miesian aesthetic went against the American grain sidesteps contradictions in America at the time. American corporations *were* extremely regimented. Individualism *was* frowned upon. The buildings of Mies and his followers capture this aspect of fifties America

were early adherents to Modernism.

Saarinen, for one, openly admitted that he craved a place in architectural history and set about developing his own personal signature in such dynamic buildings as the Ingalls Ice Hockey Rink at Yale University, the TWA terminal at Idlewild (now Kennedy) Airport in New York, and Dulles International Airport in Washington, D.C. Saarinen wanted the very form a building took to express its function. And so the swooping forms of the hockey rink were meant to convey the excitement of the sport, while the airport terminals suggested the thrill of jet travel. Unlike Mies's metaphysical propositions, these buildings spoke to people in a brash, direct, amusing way. All you had to do was look at them to know what they were saying.

Stone's conversion from Modernism had more romantic overtones. The story goes that in 1954, after falling in love with Maria Elena Torchio, Stone married her and completely abandoned his former severe architectural style. From then on, he devoted himself to the creation of such extravagantly theatrical buildings as the United States Pavilion at the 1958 Brussels World's Fair, the jewellike gas

Morris Lapidus's Fontainebleau Hotel in Miami Beach offered visitors curving forms that were sure *not* to remind them of the glass-and-steel office buildings they were vacationing from.

Courtesy of Morris Lapidus

Courtesy of Edward Durell Stone

station at Idlewild Airport, and the American Embassy in New Delhi. (Larger, gaudier works appeared in the decades that followed.) Stone became particularly addicted to the use of screenlike terrazzo and gold-leafed metal grilles on the facades of his buildings—in other words, ornamentation, which in Modern architecture was taboo.

Modernist architects, with their penchant for restraint, deplored Stone's post-Maria work. Morris Lapidus, on the other hand, received less censure for his ultra-uninhibited Miami Beach hotels, simply because no one took them seriously. How could any Miesian believe that less was more and not wince at a man who, in designing the $13 million Fontainebleau hotel, wanted to put the money "where it shows" (as Lapidus put it)? The hotel's sweeping, arc-shaped facade bore no relation to the typical, sober glass-and-steel curtain wall favored by the Modernists. And while Mies and his followers positioned their buildings so that their ideal forms would stand out with ideal clarity, Lapidus positioned his so that its shadow would never fall across the swimming pool. In the Fontainebleau, Americana, and Eden Roc hotels, Lapidus created a blatantly hedonistic architectural style, thoroughly appropriate for places where people went to have fun. He meant those hotels to look stupendous—and stupendous they were. According to a press release, "The Americana has [sic] enough stone, wire, glass, and concrete in it to build a model community of 500 ultra-modern homes with enough left over for the town's dining, shopping, and recreation areas." And then there was the "nations of the western hemisphere" theme of the Americana's interiors, each one decorated and air-conditioned to within an inch of its life.

One can argue that this sort of flashiness was fine for hotels but inappropriate for office blocks. In fact America had given birth, not long before the fifties, to a supertheatrical architectural style that seemed to lend itself very well to office buildings—that is, American Deco. But Modernist architects deplored such Deco extravagances as New York's Chrysler Building, labeling them mere gimmicks. The style was consigned to temporary oblivion during the fifties, and even those architects given to flights of fancy paid it scant attention. As for fifties-exuberant, we will never know whether it would have made for pleasing and practical office buildings, since none were ever built in that style. America's offices in the fifties were what some dubbed "hairshirt Modernism" all the way.

Fifties architectural high spirits were evident in some private homes of the decade as well. In Oklahoma architect Bruce Goff's Bavinger house and Price house, natural and industrial materials mesh in unexpected ways, and the forms themselves are highly eccentric. As we have seen in the previous chapter, Goff's houses were elaborately and exotically ornamented, evidence of the impression Wright's work had made on him. But unlike the older man, Goff always let his clients' needs take precedence over his own ego, which is why his houses, though certainly outlandish enough in appearance, always function as they should.

John Lautner received even less attention than Goff did from the Modernist architectural establishment of the 1950s. His private homes matched in extravagance those Goff designed. The Amphitheater House in Los Angeles, for instance, boasted exterior walls that could actually be swung open like doors, so that its inhabitants could take fullest advantage of the view. And the Rounded Blockhouse, in Sherman Oaks, California, featured an exaggerated curved facade of bent redwood siding. "Are residential streets to be as exuberant as today's highways lined with the fantasies of gas station and roadside nightclub?" asked one outraged writer in a 1952 issue of *House & Home* when confronted with these buildings. John Lautner's answer to that question would probably have been a resounding "yes." And with more emphasis today on alternative lifestyles for the wealthier up-scale professionals who can afford to hire adventurous architects, who knows what will come next?

There were suburbs in the United States before the 1950s, but fifties suburbs were unlike any America had ever seen. After World War II, the demand for housing was enormous. Construction had ceased almost entirely during the war years. Now many people, especially the ten million discharged from the armed forces, were obliged to double up and share cramped quarters with relatives and friends until they could find digs of their own.

As Gwendolyn Wright notes in *Building the Dream*, in 1946 the National Housing Agency had determined that America would need seventeen million new housing units in the course of the coming decade. The federal government and real estate developers met the challenge admirably. Middle-income housing policies allowed veterans to borrow the entire cost of a house without down payment. Prefabricated materials like laminated wood roofs and steel-frame wall panels with painted aluminum "clapboards" were available in abundance. Some companies were even marketing entire prefabricated houses. A 1949 housing act helped finance suburban projects, and though builders managed to manipulate this program so as to reap huge, illegal profits, the homes that people needed so desperately did get built.

Acres of land were bulldozed flat all over the country, turning virgin rural areas into grist for the developer's mill. Then up went the houses, in Panorama City, California; Lakewood, outside Los Angeles; Oak Forest near Houston; and Park Forest, thirty miles south of Chicago. Of all the fifties developments, though, perhaps none was as widely heralded as Levittown, Long Island, the work of developer William J.

Levitt. Levitt had started building there in 1945; by 1952, Levittown's population had risen to ten thousand.

The homes Levitt built could not have pleased Modern architects of the day, but certainly his preferred mode of construction would have struck a responsive chord. The houses were built according to assembly-line principles. Each nonunion worker (nonunion to keep construction costs down) was given a particular task to do, and he did it in house after house after house until the whistle blew. With these methods, Levitt could knock out 150 houses a week, and if they weren't exactly Mies van der Rohe originals, people were nevertheless lining up to buy them, preferring to live in a community that promised to be less expensive and cleaner than the deteriorating cities, as well as safer for their children.

Given the mode of production—mass production of identical structures—it is not surprising that suburban houses themselves lacked architectural distinction. In terms of style, they owed nothing whatsoever to Wright or Mies or any of the other leading architects of the 1950s, except perhaps their inclusion of open spaces and multipurpose rooms. Indeed, the Federal Housing Authority refused to finance developers whose designs they deemed too Modern-looking, assuming that it was a fad that sooner or later would pass. And so developers built ranch houses and split-levels in conservative styles they knew would appeal to both the housing authority officials and customers: Colonial, Tudor, Spanish, and Cape Cod. Leading architects could theorize all they wanted about what kind of houses they thought people ought to

live in, but these reassuringly familiar styles corresponded with most people's idea of what a home should look like. As one *Good Housekeeping* writer stated (quoted by Russell Lynes in *The Tastemakers*), fifties Americans evidently wanted "the exterior [of a suburban house] to be a contemporary treatment of some familiar architectural style [and] the interior to be the ultimate in modern convenience." Given the uniformity of these mass-produced houses, it is no wonder that fifties Americans chose such unusual color combinations for their rooms; this was one acceptable way of endowing them with a bit of individuality.

Fifties suburban homes, though unlike glass-and-steel boxes in every way, resembled them in their standardization and repetitiveness. Although some developers tried to create a sense of variety in the suburbs they built, in most cases it was a question of block after brand-new block of identical, brand-new houses. The people who lived in those houses were all-of-a-kind, too, in some ways. Indeed, in the late forties the federal government actually encouraged developers to allow members of only one or another religion or ethnic group to buy homes in their communities, although such discriminatory policies were ultimately outlawed. Still, suburban communities did tend to attract people of the same age group and social level. All were young, white newlyweds starting out, with little children and maybe another child on the way. There was no place for single people or old people or unmarried people living together—and of course there was no place in these communities for blacks or gays. Sociological studies of the decade told of all

Courtesy of the International Community Corp.

Courtesy of the International Community Corp.

the drinking that went on behind the walls of those split-levels; of the sense of dissatisfaction suburbanites felt in their newborn neighborhoods; of the side effects of living in such overly controlled environments.

Yet just as many people went on working for rigidly structured corporations, so they remained in those rigidly ordered suburbs. Life was convenient there. Soon shopping centers were built, and schools and libraries, movie theaters, and churches and synagogues, all in the boxy, low-cost, unimaginative version of Modern architecture that developers found so congenial to their bankbooks. Who could complain? Suburban life was an orderly life, a cozy life in certain ways. After the shock of World War II, nothing was more desirable for millions of Americans than order. And for those who remembered the Depression vividly, the prospect of owning one's own house was a very pleasing one.

In a sense, the very houses themselves ordered the lives of the suburbanites who lived in them. Gwendolyn Brooks observes that these houses often had few interior walls, a cost-cutting ploy that also discouraged privacy and promoted family "togetherness" (the popular term a *McCall's* editor coined in 1956). Many model suburban houses also featured built-in television units, it being assumed that no one who came to live in suburbia would want to forgo television. Houses also included a "den" of some sort, a sanctuary whither harried dad could retire after a hard day at the office; in an age when women with any career goals of their own were considered neurotic and frigid, it only figured that there was no den for mom to go to after a harder day of seeing to the house and kids.

By the end of the fifties, the once-thriving home industry began to sag. The houses developers built proved inappropriate for too many different kinds of people; not everyone who wanted to live in a house was white, under forty, middle-class, married, and had kids. Only in the 1960s, with the rise of cluster planning, was a new, less-regimented approach taken to suburban living.

Rashomon in suburbia: two views of an American suburb of the 1950s, one from the air, another—in a 1983 painting in the contemporary realist mode by David Fisch entitled *Ithaca*—from ground level. (In fact, they are not the same suburb, though they are for all intents and purposes interchangeable.) The aerial view attests to the impressively systematic approach developers of the fifties took in laying out these new neighborhoods. Fisch's painting, on the other hand, endows these neighborhood streets with a forlorn quality. The artist calls the painting "a contemplation of the original promise of the suburb that my parents' generation bought wholeheartedly."

Jeff Blechman. Courtesy of the artist David Fisch

According to Dorothy Kalins, editor-in-chief of the magazine *Metropolitan Home*, fifties tract houses like the one shown here are "the biggest building stock in the country" as of 1985. Kalins detects a trend towards renovating these properties.

GULF

On the Road

If fifties Americans ever found themselves bored by the suburbs, there was always the possibility of hopping into the car and taking a drive. By the mid-1950s, there were plenty of roads for them to do it on—and plenty of cars, too. Increased car travel brought about thousands of new roadside establishments, especially along the country's commercial strips. Fast-food restaurants, drive-in movies, bowling alleys, motels, service stations, car washes, ice-cream stands—all vied with one another for the passing motorist's at-

tention and patronship. The architects of these buildings were for the most part obscure (although John Lautner, for one, did design several Los Angeles coffee shops). Nor did their efforts interest the architectural elite of the day. Critic Rayner Banham recalls in an article in *Landscape* how the Museum of Modern Art's Arthur Drexler, while curating the ''Modern Architecture U.S.A.'' exhibit, informed him ''that people might build such things [as roadside concerns] and they might be culturally significant, but he would not

want to show them in the museum, which had always set a high valuation on 'quality' design.''

But the architects of roadside buildings were not aiming for ''quality'' design, at least not as MOMA defined it. They were aiming to sell. For that reason, they conceived their buildings as advertisements whose extravagant shapes, brilliant colors, and bright, spotless interiors would lure people off the road, out of their cars, and inside.

Both the insides and outsides of these places said ''Modern, capital

Most fifties gas stations were built in the 19_ mold and were basically white boxes. This Gulf station is exception, recalling the 1950s exuberances of architects s as Eero Saarinen and Edward Durrell Stone. Unfortunat this style never caught on, and by the sixties, the white bo had given way to little pseudo-colonial buildings.

A sign advertises a bowling alley in the latter half of fifties. Bowling, a popular pastime during that decade, now become a very ''fifties''— and increasingly fashionabl leisure-time activity.

Tim Street-Porter

Courtesy of the architect Alan Hess

Young California architect Alan Hess was clearly influenced by Los Angeles drive-in coffee shops of the fifties in his design for this newer version.

M''—but this was a decidedly different variety of Modernism than the one espoused by Mies et al. A writer in a 1952 issue of *House & Home* provided some idea of what such buildings were like in an article on so-called Googie architecture, ''named after a remarkable restaurant in Los Angeles called Googie's'' (which, incidentally, was designed by John Lautner). ''It starts off like any other building,'' the writer continued, ''but suddenly it breaks for the sky. The bright red roof of cellular steel decking suddenly tilts upward as if swung on a hinge, and the whole building goes up with it like a rocket ramp. But there is another building next door. So the flight stops as suddenly as it began.'' If Googie architecture resembled anything else happening on the American scene at the time, it was the flamboyant work of Saarinen, Wright, and Goff. On the commercial strips, though, the shapes were even more extreme—almost absurdly so, given the fact that these were fairly small, simply constructed buildings and sometimes no more than stands. Yet the roadside buildings of the fifties made up for what they lacked in size with lots of crowd-pleasing flash. And the freedom and sense of humor with which their architects manipulated the most outrageous, over-scaled forms—sleek parabolas, pylons, boomerang shapes, palette shapes, trapezoids, arrows of all kinds, soaring prow shapes, and slanting dart shapes—all of them limned, come nightfall, in neon, jutting out to grab you as you hurtled past along the highway, must have been a most refreshing change from both the monotonous glass-and-steel monoliths of the cities and the stamped-out suburban homes.

Fifties roadside buildings had a certain gratuitousness about them. But as that *House & Home* writer joked, ''Googie accustoms the people to expect strangeness, and makes them readier for those strange things yet to come which will make truly good sense.''

Art by Bob Scott

Fifties roadside eateries provided Bob Scott with the inspiration for this eighties illustration. Today's illustrators, in a satirical spirit, are given to depicting creatures of the 1950s as amiable automata like these.

Hollywood, a showplace for imaginative commercial architecture during the 1950s boasted such wonders as Pioneer Chicken; some of these nostalgic treats have gone unaltered for thirty years.

A simplified starburst-topped column and an arrow wrapping itself around what might be thought of as the state of Arkansas in reverse constitute the by-now familiar, free-standing sign, first used in 1952, of America's Holiday Inns. Note the cursive lettering, common in fifties graphics and signage, that fits in well with postwar casualness.

Tim Street-Porter

Courtesy of Holiday Inns, Inc.

Retro-Pop

Courtesy of Venturi, Rauch, and Scott Brown Architects

The architectural firm of Venturi, Rauch & Scott Brown, in their 1978 Best Products showroom in the Oxford Valley Mall in Langhorn, Pennsylvania, allude to the "dumb box" that characterized classic commercial roadside architecture in America from the 1920s up until its golden era in the fifties. Steven Izenour, an associate of the firm, notes that the approach to the building was pretty much that which a packaging designer would take to a Kleenex dispenser: "You take that box and make it 'pretty.'"

Fifties influences on today's fashion, graphics, furniture, and visual arts have a decidedly humorous, exaggerated quality to them. With architecture, however, more practical considerations prevail, limiting the architect's sense of free play. And while many of today's architects are in the process of reassessing past styles that lie outside both the mainstream of architectural history and the canons of "good taste," the various themes of the more extravagant fifties architectural trends have yet to be taken up anew on any large scale. As for the *very* mainstream Miesian aesthetic that came of age during the 1950s, it now undergoes constant criticism from those architects with so-called post-Modernist leanings, who condemn Modern architecture for its cold impersonality.

There are, however, exceptions to these trends. Here and there one can spot references to 1950s roadside buildings, especially in the occasional inclusion of free-form shapes amid elements culled from other architectural styles. And Miesian Modernism, no longer seen as an absolutist imperative but as one style among many, now offers its motifs to the few architects who feel free to blend many historical styles rather than restrict themselves to those currently in favor.

Finally, some younger architects, particularly those on the West Coast, have begun to take a closer look at fifties Pop buildings and to envision structures that do not so much parody them as arise directly from the same outlook underlying the originals. At the same time, attempts are being made to preserve those originals, which are now being recognized as important cultural artifacts. Relics of a vanished if fairly recent past, many of them are being considered more and more seriously as worthy of landmark status—and some, like the first McDonald's, may soon be awarded this designation.

Here White Castle, a popular roadside hamburger chain, blends historical styles with a fifties insouciance. This recent example is basically a box with overtones of a medieval castle and a sign whose asymmetrical quadrilateral harks back to the 1950s.

Courtesy of Coca-Cola Co.

7

Fashion

Disastrous as it was in most other respects, World War II proved to be an enormous boon to American fashion. Previously, our designers had looked to—and imitated—Paris *haute couture*. But style was not on many Parisians' minds during the German occupation, and so American fashion design had the chance to come into its own during the war years. As one editor enthused in *Harper's Bazaar* (quoted by Michael and Ariane Batterberry in *Fashion, The Mirror of History*), ''We published the New York

white or French blue dinner jackets. The typical black dinner jacket would be worn with a narrow bow tie, a starched white shirt, and black patent leather pumps—nothing unusual there.

At the same time, the decade's top designers created evening dresses that were anything but dull. ''Romantic and ladylike,'' Quentin Bell calls them in *On Human Finery*. Their colors varied. Black and white were fine for fall and winter, as were reds, browns, and beiges. Come summer, hues became

Evening

Openings with pride in the achievements of our American Designs. We have learned from the greatest masters of fashion in the world. Learned, then added something of our own. Such clothes have never been made in America before.'' Fashion magazines do have a way of exaggerating, but that much was certainly true.

The designers who rose to prominence in those years—among them Norman Norell, Hattie Carnegie, Russian-Jewish emigré Pauline Trigère, ex-American-in-Paris Mainbocher, James Galanos, Arnold Scaasi, and Gilbert Adrian—went on to become the leading lights in American high fashion during the fifties. Some designed only for a select clientele. Others offered their costly ready-to-wear creations to a wilder but equally well-heeled public. But all provided images of ultimate glamour and sophisticated romance that rivaled Paris fashion in both imagination and luxury.

We sometimes tend to view the fifties as a decade of drab conformity. In fact, men's formal wear of the period was rather unexciting. It consisted mainly of natural-shouldered, shawl-collared black dinner jackets and trousers or, for summer or the tropics,

exotic, with yellow, lime, orange, coral, and turquoise. Insofar as materials went, silk crepe was favored, as were lace, taffeta, stiff satin, and rustling brocade. Synthetics—particularly rayon and rayon blends—were by no means shunned. Postwar ''miracle'' fibers offered the ability to hold a shape, which was taken advantage of by high-fashion designers and clothing mass-manufacturers alike. Today synthetics might strike us as tacky or at best prosaic, but in the 1950s, designers worked them into opulent creations of such poetry that their unromantic origin in a vat of bubbling liquid plastic was forgotten.

Modern functionality and simplicity were the watchwords for most fifties design, whether it was a magazine layout, a chair, or a skyscraper. But women's high-style evening wear of the period was somewhat anomalous in its complicated construction, its urbane air, and in a decade of mass fashion, its exclusivity.

The evening gowns of these years ranged from long, full-skirted affairs to long, narrow sheaths. Short, full-skirted cocktail dresses, ethereal confections of double-layered chiffon, were also worn after sunset. A full

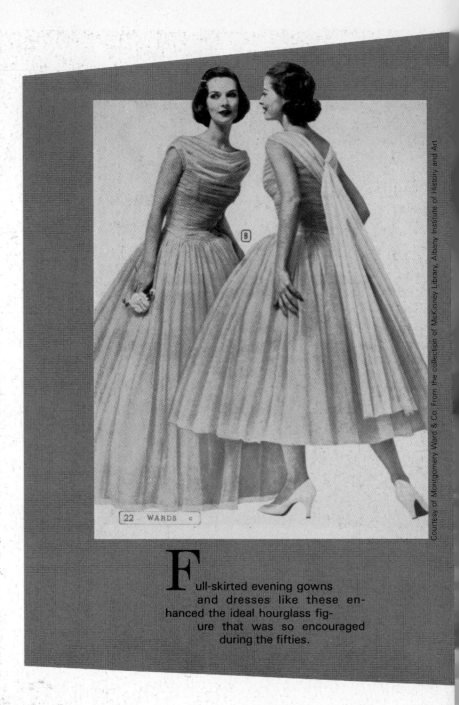

Full-skirted evening gowns and dresses like these enhanced the ideal hourglass figure that was so encouraged during the fifties.

Maverick designer Charles James created this evening gown *(left)* for Dupont.

Fashion designer Janet Russo's 50s/80s cocktail dress *(above)* boasts full skirts that evoke the fifties originals. Note this illustration's intentionally naïve style. The figure recalls the sort of Barbie-esque prom queens little girls once got together and sketched on afternoons after school.

Sartorially speaking, fifties evening wear for men placed them very much in the background. Her simple cocktail sheath and pearls could not have been more appropriate for the occasion depicted in this ad *(left)*.

Norman Norell's sequinned creations *(right)* of the 1950s had a martini-dry, worldly quality that reappears in many different guises in the decade's furniture, fabric designs, and graphics.

skirt, whether long or short, concealed a woman's body below her waistline and helped emphasize big, rounded hips, an essential feature which, along with big breasts and narrow-waist, constituted the ideal hourglass figure, that epitome of femininity homecoming soldiers evidently craved. The long sheaths, on the other hand, molded to a woman's contours—or rather, to the contours created by the figure-controlling all-in-one corselet she would have worn to give herself the wasp waist, slim hips, and uplifted breasts also considered desirable during the fifties. These dresses were tightly fitted and often sleeveless,

strapless, or cut revealingly low, and they often boasted elaborate inner foundations to give the "perfect" figure to women who did not have it naturally. Plunging backlines made quite a stir as well. "They dive as far as the wearer dares," one *Life* reporter observed, "for a public grown jaded on strapless tops and plunging necklines." A straight little waist-length dangle jacket might figure into the scheme of things, or perhaps an evening sweater, especially if it was highlighted with beads or embroidery and worn with some fabulous brooch.

Designer Norell, for one, believed that while a woman should look sub-

dued by day, she must *blossom* at night. Most other high-style designers of the 1950s evidently agreed, for their evening wear had little to do with daily life and everything to do with dreams. An urban socialite might choose to look cool and icy in a severely elegant Mainbocher or devil-may-care in a sequinned Traina-Norell sheath. For the young and chic there were clean-lined, floor-length culottes by Trigère; for the madly flamboyant, printed silk dresses by Galanos. Of course, these dubious stereotypes have little to do with what women were really like. But fifties high-style designers did not want reality. They wanted drama. And their

work *was* strong and dramatic, never saccharine or sentimental.

In the realm of accessories, fur stoles, cloth wraps, and capes abounded, serving to further heighten the sense of drama. Gloves varied in length, but whether in fabric or in doeskin they were always *de rigueur*. Handbags and slim-lined satin pumps matched the dress. A really adventurous woman might even color her hair so that it, too, would match her evening clothes; she could choose from a wide spectrum of natural and decidedly unnatural hues, thanks to the many available hair-coloring products. Even more thoroughgoing color coorination would have included matching nail polish, mascara, lustrous eyeshadow, and lining pencil, with perhaps an undercoating of colored face powder (pale blue for blondes, subtle green for redheads, soft yellow for brunettes, pastel pink for the gray-haired) before the flesh-toned, neutral powder went on.

The decade's most fashionable women tended to wear their hair short and swept back off their faces. Coiffures were curly but not at all natural-looking, and they were made possible only with curlers, rollers, and permanent waves, as well as with frequent trips to the beauty salon. Because hair-styles were short, cosmetics seemed especially necessary. Come evening, they were frequently used to create a stylized look distinguished early in the decade, by arched eyebrows, dark lips, and doe eyes and by bright lips and softer eyes later on.

So that her face might not appear unbecomingly bare, a woman, when she was going out for the evening, would have worn chandelier earrings or large, lightweight gold balls, and perhaps a long necklace—nothing excessive. Sparkling, yes, but elegantly restrained. A woman with avant-garde sympathies might have opted for a piece of the one-of-a-kind craft jewelry so popular at the time. Costume jewelry was also acceptable with even the most lavish outfits.

The strongest influence on American high style of the 1950s may have been French designer Christian Dior, whose 1947 ''New Look'' had a galvanic effect on fashion in both the United States and Europe. The widely lauded and eagerly followed work of Balenciaga and Balmain also proved catalytic here. But during the fifties, American fashion designers struck out on paths of their own and provided wealthy women with a viable alternative to Parisian couturiers. Their clothing, of course, was for an elite who had the money to buy it and the places to go to show it off. The majority of American women, however, followed these fashions in magazines such as *Vogue* and the stunningly designed *Harper's Bazaar,* in whose pages the young Richard Avedon captured the worldly elegance that epitomized fifties high style. Should less monied women go out for the evening, there were always the less pricey knockoffs to be had, in which they, too, could experience all the drama and excitement fifties high style promised. There was also the even cheaper New Look-influenced clothes that were worn by the vast majority of women.

The Kobal Collection

Are *sequins* a girl's best friend? The sequins here *(left)* are hard and slippery to the touch. The gowns they spangle cling to the body revealingly.

Graphic designer Jim Heimann offsets fifties frivolity (as embodied by the gowned woman and the car) with fifties angst (as embodied by those menacing UFOs).

Art by Jim Heimann

The Man in the Gray Flannel Suit

American women's high fashion of the 1950s was pricey, but under its glamorous spell the wearer swiftly lost touch with the workaday world where the money to buy those costly clothes was earned. Women blessed with large disposable incomes could afford to emerge into the night as fantastic creatures, gorgeously gowned and elegantly coiffed. But the money they paid for those gowns did not come from the same airy realm that they seemed to inhabit. It came from a more mundane region—a region whose inhabitants for the most part wore gray flannel suits and worked, for the most part, in large corporations.

Sloane Wilson's 1955 novel *The Man in the Gray Flannel Suit* provided America with a new stereotype: the corporate executive who chose to do everything by the rules, who was content—or *tried* to be content— working within a corporate structure rather than striking out bravely on his own. Gone were the rugged individualists and visionary tycoons of yesteryear. Conformity and rigid hierarchies were the orders of the day, especially in the business world. Sinister though they might seem today, at the time they served as an effective antidote to the disorienting jolts and upsets caused by World War II. So long as conformity was the order of the day, there was a uniform to go with it: a three-button, single-breasted, char-

coal gray flannel suit, with narrow shoulders, narrow, small-notched lapels, flaps on the pockets, and pleatless, tapering trousers. A white or pale blue cotton broadcloth shirt with a button-down collar and button cuffs, trim ties with regimental stripes and small knots, and trim, black leather shoes that rose at the ankle and tapered at the toe—these, too, were essential ingredients. A drip-dry beige raincoat, a Chesterfield with black velvet collar, or a single-breasted, straight-lined tweed overcoat with raglan sleeves was donned upon stepping out of corporate headquarters and onto the street. Any hat would have been narrow-brimmed and worn brim up or brim down, sometimes with a pinched crown. Hair was worn in a short crew- or semicrew- cut. Jewelry was minimal—no more than a wristwatch and, if the man was married, a wedding band. This style of dressing had originated at least three decades before, among wealthy Ivy Leaguers. By the mid-1950s, however, the look was cropping up all over America and not only among the preppie set.

The ideal gray flannel suiter was tall and trim. Dressed in his uniform, he stood out neither in a crowd nor at work. Nor was he meant to. At big corporations, anonymity was preferred. During World War II, those corporations had obtained hefty government contracts. By the fifties they

were technologically way ahead of smaller companies that had had neither the opportunities nor the funds to carry on the large-scale research and development on which big business had thrived during the war years. In the 1950s, big corporations got even bigger, employed more and more people, and became more complex. These vast, impersonal enterprises had no need for individualistic men who would stick out of the crowd, sartorially or otherwise. They needed pawns they could move easily from one part of the country to another without having to think too hard about who that pawn was. The gray flannel suit look provided just the right touch of anonymity. It was the corporate style par excellence, the clothing counterpart of the anonymous glass-and-steel box corporate headquarters built during the decade.

But it would be over-generalizing to say that men worked in nothing but gray flannel suits during the fifties. Factory workers did not wear them, of course, although with cleaner, safer factory conditions, blue-collar laborers were often able to work in sports clothes rather than overalls. And even in the business world, there were alternatives to the prevailing charcoal gray. By the mid-1950s, clothes made of lightweight, spot- and crease-resistant synthetics were bought and worn by both men and women. Suits in nubby

Courtesy of Montgomery Ward & Co. From the collection of McKinney Library, Albany Institute of History and Art

* Lucky the man!

Coat **12.75** Slacks **6.85** Outfit **19.25**

Coat **19.95** Slacks **7.70** Outfit **26.95**

silklike synthetics and rayon and Dacron blends became popular in beige, blue, brown, elephant gray, and a black with a goldish sheen to it. Other suits and overcoats were enlivened by the not-very-lively sounding slubs, random flecks of brightly colored fabric that tempered the sober palette of 1950s menswear. Synthetic seersucker put in an appearance as well, especially in the summer months, and quickly lost its strictly upper-class connotations. And in 1956, shapely two-buttoned suits in worsted fabrics from Italy found their way to these shores, soon to be imitated and modified by American manufacturers pushing the "Continental" look. That look featured broad shoulders, a shaped waistline, and dress shirts with rounded collars, all of which offered a contrast to the trim, gray-flannel-suit silhouette.

Reflecting the modest variety of business clothes they had available to them, during the fifties men tended to care far less about fashion than women did. As an article in a 1957 issue of *Newsweek* had it, "men prefer to spend the extra money they're earning on things other than clothes," namely their homes and growing families, and the men's clothing industry had the dismaying statistics to prove it. The blandest attire was adequate for work. Men did not have to worry about keeping up with the changing styles for the simple reason that, in men's clothes, the styles did not change as noticeably from year to year as they did in women's fashion. In fact, the one area where fifties American men seemed to exhibit any fashion consciousness at all was in that of sports clothes. Only on weekends or on holiday did men let themselves go a bit with these clothes which, while not exactly flamboyant, had more character than typical weekday apparel.

If men's suits tended to be conservative in the fifties, sports jackets and slacks had a jauntier air, as is evident from this page *(left)* in a 1958 Montgomery Ward catalog. Today, countless vintage clothing shops carry items like these, which have been incorporated into the sartorial style of young New Wavers.

In the film version of *The Man in the Gray Flannel Suit*, Gregory Peck *(right)* was the eponymous hero.

The Kobal Collection

Leisure time gave men more opportunities for self-expression in fashion. Devotion to work was one way of living up to the American ideal; making the most of one's leisure time was another. America's enterprising capitalists during the fifties convinced consumers that each one of life's occasions called for one or more purchases. And so, just as there were clothes one simply *had* to buy for work, there were mandatory outfits for having fun in, too: that is, sports clothes.

There were appropriate sports

muda shorts some men favored in these years, going so far as to wear them out to the country club with sports jackets, the obligatory knee-length socks, and tasseled slip-on shoes.

If the occasion were less dressy, a pair of trousers or shorts and a sport shirt would do. Long- or short-sleeved sport shirts, many in lightweight, washable, wrinkle-free synthetics like Dacron, were available in numerous patterns—checks, stripes, plaids, paisleys, and foulards—perhaps with

Sporty

clothes for all manner of casual occasions. Most formal were the sports jackets and slacks which offered, as one writer put it, "Ease and Naturalness . . . No Exaggeration . . . Distinction without Drabness . . . and comfort via lighter weight apparel" (quoted by Schoeffler and Gale in *Esquire's Encyclopedia of 20th Century Men's Fashions*). Sports jackets—single-breasted, with a single vent—came in colorful madras plaids (a prerogative of Palm Beach tycoons that filtered down to the masses), loud checks or smaller-scaled houndstooth checks, and windowpanes. The more conservative dressers opted for lustrous navy blue jackets of silk or silklike synthetics, or black ones flecked with colorful slubs. For cooler climes, there were jackets in popular pinwhale corduroy. Like the suits of the period, these jackets had natural shoulders and straight-hanging backs. Cuffless, slim-cut, matching slacks were worn with a trim belt. They came in white as well as a host of snappy coordinating colors. Indeed, as a 1958 issue of *Esquire* declared, "the brighter the trousers, the better to relax in a holiday mood." More casual were the Ber-

an embroidered monogram or crest enlivening the breast pocket, recalling Queen Elizabeth's 1953 coronation which so fascinated fifties Americans. These shirts offered relief from the work week's white or pale blue cotton broadcloth. Even at their brightest, though, sport shirts still had a muted look to them. However, zany Hawaiian "aloha" shirts with jazzy floral patterns or Polynesian motifs proved an exception to this rule and echoed the exaggeratedly exotic spirit of some of the home furnishings and interior design of the period.

There was sporty men's outerwear as well. During the war, some of the manufacturers under contract to the government had done intensive research into and development of waterproof and lightweight fabrics that would provide as much warmth as heavier fabrics. When it seemed as if the Japanese would block America's access to Australian wool, a viable synthetic substitute for that fiber was sought as well. When the war ended, clothing manufacturers were quick to apply wartime technological developments to civilian clothes.

Men's sports outerwear ranged

What did the man in the gray flannel suit wear when he was on vacation? Maybe one of these splendid Hawaiian shirts *(above),* whose gaudy colors and intricate patterns have yet to go out of fashion.

Courtesy of Anheuser-Busch, Inc.

Boxer-type swimming trunks were well-suited to the ideal male figure of the fifties, which was fuller and bulkier than today's.

In men's bathing suits of the 1950s, deep-toned, ''masculine'' solids and plaids prevailed. Contemporary graphic artist Jim Heimann endows these *Three Divers (right)* with the greyhound grace of the eighties.

ven men's sports shirts with less high-spirited patterns those enlivening the Hawaiian shirts of the fifties ted subtle, intriguing designs. The circles, elongated gles, and asymmetrical quadrilaterals on this one seem ve escaped from a 1930s Kandinsky abstraction. Today, ar shapes frequently show up in New Wave graphics.

from the suave, belted storm coat with pile fabric collar to the plainer, knee-length, loden cloth duffle coat, with its big patch pockets and detachable hood that was held closed by wooden toggles and hemp loops rather than a zipper or buttons. The thigh-length ''car'' coat was also popular, especially among suburbanites. But perhaps the most well-known and most relaxed piece of men's outerwear was the one made famous by that most relaxed of American presidents, Ike Eisenhower: the jaunty, blousy, waist-length ''Eisenhower'' jacket. Come winter, headgear such as knit stocking

caps (known in my day as ''poopkie'' hats), Russian fur caps, and billed caps with lined earflaps completed the outfit. In addition, there were also rough-and-ready plaid wool shirts in deep reds, blues, and greens that were warm, rugged, and perfect for the fall. Cardigans and zipper-front sweaters in muted tones with a few bright highlights also helped keep fifties outdoors people warm.

In the fifties, thanks to mass-produced clothing, both middle-class and working-class men could approximate one another in terms of attire. Higher salaries enabled both to enjoy

the same pastimes as well. And so, as the mercury rose, similarly garbed middle- and working-class men headed for the golf course, patio, or beach. The sportswear they wore was decidedly informal: short-sleeved, knitted T-shirts; gabardine or twill slacks; and trunk-type bathing suits in sober-hued solids, small plaids, or stripes. Increased affluence during the 1950s also meant increased traveling, by car and airplane, and so these sporty, lightweight duds were as likely to be seen at a Grosse Pointe country club as in the purlieu of a Miami Beach hotel pool.

Women by Day

Courtesy of Montgomery Ward & Co. From the collection of McKinney Library, Albany Institute of History and Art

While some women's fashions changed radically from year to year during the fifties, the shirtwaist dress remained a constant. It was—and still is to many women—the suburban outfit par excellence. Although the style has changed slightly, the dress is made to look neat all day. Patterns were and are often small-scaled or solid.

Courtesy of Montgomery Ward & Co. From the collection of McKinney Library, Albany Institute of History and Art

Though less essential than they were in the 1940s, hats were thought of as only appropriate for formal occasions during the 1950s. According to a 1959 survey, the "average American woman" owned four of them.

Neiman Marcus featured this smart-looking suit designed by David Hayes. The bright, hard colors are definitely eighties, but the dangle jacket and cocked pillbox hat recall sophisticated women's day wear of the 1950s.

Depending on where they were and what they were doing, American women during the 1950s had the opportunity to look either as bland and conservative as the men or somewhat looser and more at ease. For most career women, though, wool suits—especially those in sharkskin or worsted flannel—were the norm. As with much women's evening wear, the ideal silhouette was long-legged and wasp-waisted—a silhouette realized thanks to the slim sheath skirts cut to the knee and the straight, short, soft-shouldered jackets (collarless or with little fur collars) that went over silk blouses.

To maintain that slim, simple silhouette, women watched their weight and/or wore girdles and kept accessories to a minimum. Jewelry was limited to no more than simple earrings, an enameled or jeweled brooch, and if the woman was married, a wedding ring. Gloves, however, were a must. A woman dressed in a suit would never go out without them, lest she be obliged, in the course of her peregrinations, to shake hands with a man who might interpret the touch of her bare skin as a sexual come-on. Hats, too, were essential. Some were quite large, but the most characteristic ones, created by master milliners like John Frederics and Mr. John, were small, pert, brimless pillboxes or berets, or else unusual creations with asymmetrical brims and bits of veil or feathery ornamentation that were to be worn tilted to the side. The curious "wizard's" caps were also chic, though they had a way of giving women an oddly wraithlike appearance. Handbags in vividly colored lizardskin or leather harmonized with the suit. The matching shoes were usually quite narrow and often boasted cruelly high, thin stiletto heels.

Weather permitting, all this would be enfolded in a polo coat, which came in materials ranging from plain cloth to iridescent "poodle" cloth (named after the most popular breed of dog in the fifties), to camel's hair, cashmere, or luxurious vicuña. These coats were usually straight and fell to just below the knee.

As interpreted by a multitude of designers including Ben Zuckerman, Adele Simpson, Leonard Arkin, David Crystal, Jonny Herbert, Bonnie Cashin, Claire McCardell, Henry Rosenfeld, and Nettie Rosenstein—as well as those unsung opportunists who were influenced by their designs—the well-dressed 1950s career woman's suit and coat gave her a long, carved appearance that, like the swankier look of evening fashions, bespoke not sensuality but a certain worldliness. It was as if these efficient modern ladies simply had no time or patience for anything fussy or excessive, including sex.

Which is not to say that women's daywear of that decade was not *adult*. It was. For these clothes were never cloying or girlishly cute. Rather, there was something intriguingly dry and cool about them (a dryness and lack of warmth evident in the more austere fifties furniture as well). The tall, lean American models of the period (of whom Suzy Parker was perhaps the best known) were young, of course, but not especially joyous or youthful. They often assumed angular, slightly startled poses in the fashion plates, while their facial expressions communicated something between archness and an ironic detachment that tingled with a hint of high-voltage tension. It was as if, after Hitler and Hiroshima, these women were alert, yes, but past worrying, past caring, and only mildly curious to see what the future would bring. Their beauty was mild, too: unethnic, cool, refined, and never earthy or (heaven forbid!) vulgar. What's more, their bearing made it clear that the clothes they wore were definitely not for daddy's little girl or the country mouse but for women of the postwar world.

Less formal than these suits were "separates." Separates consisted of tops (tight, sometimes sleeveless and collarless; quasi-leotards; cardigans; and wool jersey blouses) and skirts (full or pleated) that could be combined at will, thereby providing a woman with a variety of outfits at a lower cost. Maverick designer Claire McCardell is credited with having created separates after growing tired of traveling around the world with a steamer trunk and heaps of suitcases. Perhaps more than any designer of the 1950s, it was McCardell who emphasized functionality and simplicity in her clothes (two qualities that furniture designers and architects of the fifties emphasized as well). Unlike most of her contemporaries, she more or less ignored Paris, finding inspiration in her native land instead. "It's freedom, it's democracy, it's casualness, it's good health," McCardell declared. "Clothes can say all that"—and her clothes did, whether they were dressy suits in shocking pink or red-and-black tweed

with short jackets and slim or full skirts, or the more casual and phenomenally popular sportswear that became synonymous with the "American Look" of the fifties. Comfortable and easy-fitting, McCardell's separates—as well as many of her other designs—met with a warm response from American women, who found their clean lines timeless.

Both full-skirted shirtwaist dresses, high-waisted dresses reminiscent of the Empire style, and wool jumpers all added to the list of daywear possibilities for women. McCardell designed

these as well, as did numerous other designers of both pricier garments and cheaper imitations. Unlike the sheath skirts of the decade, these were relatively comfortable to wear (though here, too, unless the dress was high-waisted, narrow waists were essential, especially when played up with a wide, tight, "important" belt), and they were appropriate for both the career "gal" on the go and the suburban housewife with a carload of kids to chauffeur around.

The biggest news in fifties women's daywear was made by the chemise,

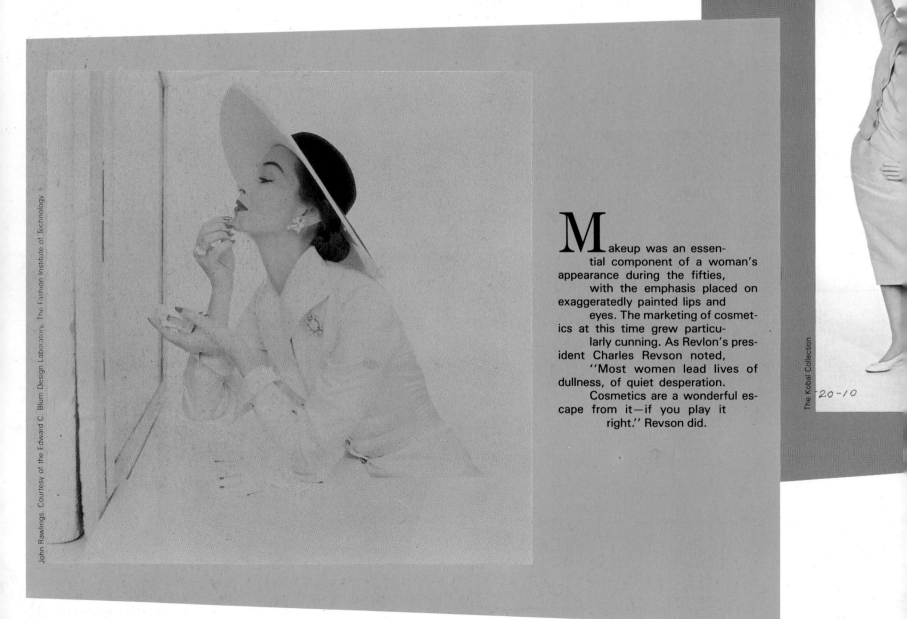

20-10

Makeup was an essential component of a woman's appearance during the fifties, with the emphasis placed on exaggeratedly painted lips and eyes. The marketing of cosmetics at this time grew particularly cunning. As Revlon's president Charles Revson noted, "Most women lead lives of dullness, of quiet desperation. Cosmetics are a wonderful escape from it—if you play it right." Revson did.

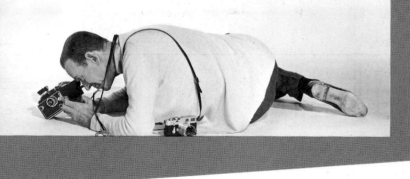

John Rawlings. Courtesy of the Edward C. Blum Design Laboratory, The Fashion Institute of Technology

This clutch coat was distinguished by dolman sleeves and an extravagant shawl collar. There are no buttons, which is why the model is clutching it closed. A coat like this was deemed suitable for both day *and* evening—a rare instance of versatility in a decade addicted to rigid rules and regulation as to when an article of clothing could or could not be worn.

so known as the sack dress, or more bluntly, the bag, that was all the rage in 1957. Slim sheath skirts and wasp waists may have been uncomfortable, but most people felt that the chemise went too far to the opposite extreme. It was cut to just below the knee, but while the legs were visible, hips and bust were completely hidden, much to the chagrin of the American male. The chemise's "free form" (a term that would recur in regard to some 1950s home furnishings) had originated in Paris and was perhaps best explained by the French couturier Givenchy (quoted by Eve Merriam in *Figleaf*): "It is inspired . . . by modern art, the experimental art that seeks new shapes and forms, transgressing the limitations set by convention. With my new dress form I have discarded, among other things, the limitations set by the shape of the female figure itself." American fashion magazines touted this unflattering creation ceaselessly, but by 1958 women decided that they had had it. They had let their imaginations be fired (some might say put themselves at the mercy of) by the fashion editors and clothing manufacturers, but *enough was enough.* By 1958 the sack was sacked.

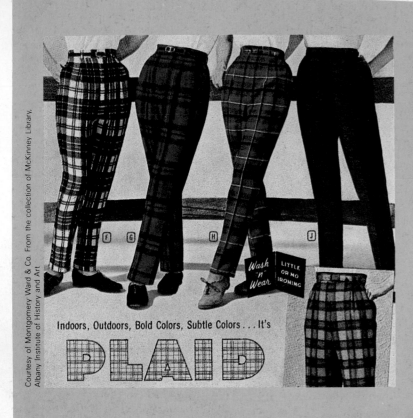

Indoors, Outdoors, Bold Colors, Subtle Colors . . . It's

PLAID

Wash "n" Wear

LITTLE OR NO IRONING

Fifties fashion was notorious for strictly classifying dress as male or female. But, by the end of the decade, slacks—a.k.a. trousers—once the sole prerogative of men and boys, had become acceptable for girls and women, too.

Bright colors and peppy patterns enlivened women's sportswear during the fifties. Fabrics for outfits like these would have been nonwrinkling, making them easy to wear and less stiff-looking than more businesslike day wear.

"The American Look"

Try as they would, men's clothing manufacturers found it hard to excite their potential customers about fashion during the 1950s. Even the men's informal sportswear of those years, while practical and comfortable, failed to generate much enthusiasm. Sportswear for women, on the other hand, was constantly making fashion headlines. The designers of menswear remained unheralded, if not altogether obscure, but American designers of women's sportswear were hailed as revolutionaries of sorts.

The sportswear of those years epitomized the so-called American Look introduced by Claire McCardell and a number of other designers. The American Look was primarily a homegrown phenomenon. However, it managed to toss off references to styles as diverse as Austrian peasant dirndls, Navajo work skirts, and French sailors' shirts—garments of ethnic lower classes rather than the nobility, and therefore fitting models for a democratic style aimed at a broad public. American Look clothes were mass-produced, simply constructed, clean-lined, durable (especially those made with synthetics), and despite their usually narrow waists, easy to wear. They were intended not so much for work as for leisure—but a leisure, as one *Time* writer noted in a 1956 cover story on McCardell, "of action—barbecue parties in the backyard, motor trips along country roads, weekend golf and water skiing." In fact, a woman could wear American Look sports clothes for any number of activities, from driving the kids to Little League practice to buying milk to running over to a friend's for a game of mah-jongg—or for that matter, to going to certain jobs—without her outfit ever looking inappropriate. Sports clothes were even acceptable for evenings, especially once group television-watching at home became a popular mode of socializing.

That these clothes were ladylike rather than blatantly sexy is not surprising, designed as they were in an era that was ignorant of open marriage and wife-swapping parties and that

saw sex as part of a romantic scenario leading inevitably to a faithful marriage. Such sportswear had a wholesome, casual air to it. Far less restrained than career women's daywear, it was nevertheless quite neat and tidy since "presentability," as the Ewens observed in *Channels of Desire,* "imposed its tyranny on manicured lawns, and, more and more, on manicured people." This was especially true in suburbia where sportswear was in such demand. Other commentators have seen the simplicity of fifties American women's sportswear as symbolic of emotionless efficiency, the female equivalent of the gray flannel suit.

But the women who embraced the American Look did not perceive it as emotionlessly efficient or cruelly tyrannical. Yes, one might say that television and magazines pushed these clothes on women. And, as Eve Merriam wrote in *Figleaf* regarding the fifties, "we have become more susceptible to conformism in fashion than at any period of history before." But women had to wear *something,* and fifties women found sportswear functional, colorful, and affordable.

Women's sportswear—jersey jumpers; trim, tailored slacks; playshorts; playsuits; Bermuda shorts; housedresses; and belted, short-sleeved golf dresses—was also comfortable. It made life that much simpler for the young, servantless, child- and chore-burdened housewives of those baby-boom years. Mix-and-match separates—a madras skirt topped, perhaps, with a simple tailored blouse boasting a Peter Pan collar, or a dirndl skirt worn with a peasant blouse—were prominent in the sportswear market, too. These, however, were not as casual as dungarees, which were only worn around the house. Other women's sportswear emphasized whimsy over function, as in the "conversation circle" (so called because whoever wore it always started people talking about her, or at least about her dress), a wide felt skirt decorated, as one *Life* reporter noted, "with anything from families of fur poodles to rhinestone telephone numbers."

Blouse, hoop earrings, wide belt (tiny wasp waist), wide, flowing skirt: During the fifties, Doris Day embodied the perfect all-American woman.

The Kobal Collection

here's the Beaver? From the ever-popular television series, "Leave It to Beaver," we have Mrs. Cleaver, in shirtwaist dress popular during the fifties, and Mr. Cleaver dressed in a short-sleeved, good-for-around-the-house polo shirt and slacks. Wally is in his chinos and T-shirt.

Sporty outerwear for women—car coats and short "toppers" cut to just below the waist—shared the practicality of men's outerwear. Ponchos and shawls were also worn, their designs often betraying the Mexican influence that was evident in many fifties home-furnishings textiles. The simple, rope-soled sandals that offset much summer sportswear also hinted of sunny Mexico, whose air of relaxed sensuality no doubt appealed to a generation of Americans who saw themselves as aspiring to the relaxed, "good life" and heading toward a sunny future. (This attitude—and its accompanying fashions—are still evident today.) For cool weather there were sweater sets, that is, a short-sleeved or sleeveless

sweater with a matching cardigan worn over it, the most coveted of which were cashmere or angora.

Swimwear fashions for women were way ahead of those for men, in terms of both stylishness and sexiness: body-hugging stretch nylon maillots; short-skirted, dresslike bathing suits; and, eventually, bikinis. The fifties bikinis were not as revealing as today's. At the time, though, they were thought of as risqué, although they were no more than modified (that is, prudish) versions of the originals first seen on the French Riviera. Prudishness notwithstanding, Rudi Gernreich, later famed for his topless bathing suit, did manage to design women's swimsuits during the fifties

that had no lining "in the interest of freedom" (as Barbara Walz notes in *The Fashion Makers*). As for the prolific McCardell, she designed a particularly odd bathing suit for women that looked a bit like a deflated cloth egg. It did little for the figure but played up what would ideally be long, slender legs. Bright, sunny days both on and off the beach called for sunglasses, especially the fanciful ones imported from Italy that were soon copied by American manufacturers. Veritable sculptures for the face, they bring to mind the decade's more extreme accessories as well as the harlequin look that enlivened some rooms.

More than any other aspect of 1950s fashion design, it is women's

sportswear that is most infused with the optimistic, democratic spirit that often informs the fifties style. Its simple outlines, intended for women bent on having a simple, good time, stemmed from the same kind of thinking that underlay so much graphic, product, furniture, and interior design of the period. All conveyed a similar message—that is, if we keep everything simple, casual, and under control, we'll be able to go on having as much fun as we're having now in this fine democracy of ours. Evidently, this outlook struck many people—especially some young ones—as overly rigid, to judge from the astonishing reaction to it in the following decade's youth revolution.

Compared to today's women's scanty bikini bottoms, this fifties one-piece number, with its built-in "panel," seems terribly confining.

Richard Litt

Part of the American Look has remained ageless; western wear, as much a style of the eighties as it was of the fifties, focuses this Richard Litt photograph. Although the setting is modern, the background and the car could easily have appeared in a similar photograph taken in earlier decades.

Courtesy of Cole of California

With fifties prosperity in full swing, American clothing manufacturers discovered—or, if you like, created, and/or exploited—new markets eager to buy their goods: children and teenagers. Between printed advertisements and television, America's young were instilled with consumerism at an early age—a consumerism far more insatiable than that of their parents, who still remembered the importance of being thrifty from their Depression days. If junior consumers were not old enough to go out and shop for them-

Kids

selves, it was highly probable that, with enough nagging, mommy or daddy would go out and buy it for them. As financial columnist Sylvia Porter remarked (quoted by Paul Sann in *Fads, Follies and Delusions of the American People*), ''The youngsters always have had a vital influence over the family's spending habits—but now even the pre-reading ones are developing definite buying habits. We're creating a nation of spenders from infancy.''

Teenagers could do their own shopping. As one executive of a large St. Louis department store put it, teenagers of the fifties ''know exactly what they want, brook no argument, buy it—bingo, like that—and depart.'' A fifteen-year-old Los Angeles girl quoted in the same 1957 article in *Newsweek* put it more succinctly: ''We just find it neat to spend money''—$9 billion of it to be precise, the figure that was cited as teenagers' disposable income in 1957.

American manufacturers did not need to read *Newsweek* to find this out. Intensive research into the hitherto untapped teen market had been going on since early in the decade. By the midfifties, manufacturers had their

Courtesy of Montgomery Ward & Co. From the collection of McKinney Library, Albany Institute of History and Art

3.98—4.98
100% Nylon

Stiff petticoats *(left)* kept little girls' skirts pleasingly full. These cumbersome garments also attempted to keep the little girls who wore them from romping around with the boys—another instance where fifties clothes reinforced traditional sex roles.

Two collegians enjoy America's favorite soft drink back in the fabulous fifties. It is easy enough to make fun of this image, yet it is also easy to see how effective a selling tool it was. Here, everyday American life is idealized and the product takes on the quality of a magic elixir.

Share

enjoy a C
in all the v

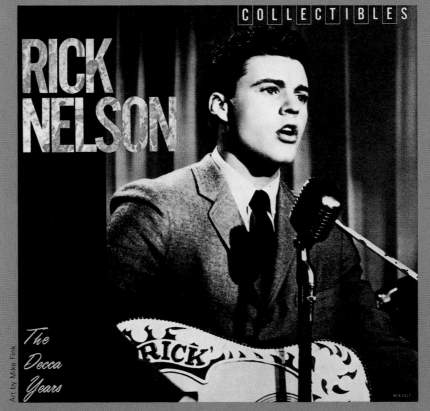

COLLECTIBLES

RICK NELSON

Art by Mike Fink

The Decca Years

RICK'

Rick Nelson, heartthrob of the late fifties, favored a clean-cut look of which few adults would have disapproved. One imagines that the teenage boys who adopted this mode of dress were not as boring as they looked. Today, a guy who dresses this way is cool.

teen-manipulating skills down to a fine art. As one ad exec saw it, teenage problems included "Keeping my temper...Worry about little things... Can't help daydreaming...Have a crush...Do things I later regret... Feel I'm not as smart as others...Get stage fright before a group...Want to gain or lose weight...Want to improve posture or bodybuild...Want to get rid of pimples...Seldom have dates...Don't have girl/boy friend... Want more people to like me...Want to make friends...Need to develop self-confidence." What conclusion did the ad exec draw from all this? "If this list doesn't make them perfect prospects for the fashion, cosmetic and allied industries—I don't know what does!"

Regardless of advertising, however, boys, like men, were usually not very interested in fashion during the fifties. Dungarees and chinos were their trousers of choice. (A 1956 *Consumer Reports* noted that Levi's, at $3.89 a pair and guaranteed to shrink to a tight fit, were most popular.) Shorts were fine for summer, while trunk-type bathing suits with patterns ranging from the nautical to the geometric were worn to the beach or pool. Dressy occasions required a sports jacket and slacks, one in a solid fabric, the other in a houndstooth or a check or plaid in deep blues, greens, grays, browns, and maroons, with hints of brighter color to liven up these sober hues. Small-collared plaid, small paisley, or striped shirts with Gay Nineties overtones, horizontally striped polo and T-shirts, and turtlenecks coordinated with the slacks, chinos, or dungarees. Sneakers, loafers, desert boots, or white bucks completed the outfit. Outerwear ranged from smaller versions of the duffle coats men also wore to high school baseball jackets with leather sleeves. The most common haircuts— common, that is, among the "good" kids, not the troublemakers—were the flattop, crew, and semi-crew cuts, or else modified ducktails, or the long-but-not-too-long, carefully combed and parted, wholesome-looking rocker hairstyles favored by such teen trendsetters as Ricky Nelson of "Ozzie and Harriet" fame.

Teenage girls, on the other hand, were positively fascinated by clothes and cosmetics and spent their money accordingly. Sheath skirts were thought of as primarily for mature women (the over-twenty crowd) and were, as a 1953 *Life* article put it, "far too confining for dances like the bunny hop, a current campus craze." According to Ellen Melinkoff's *What We Wore*, teenage girls preferred the full-skirted look that featured a four-foot-diameter skirt with plenty of petticoats underneath to puff it out and a hoop sewn into the skirt's hem to keep it nice and circular, topped with a white blouse. Box-pleated plaid skirts offered an alternative to these awkward hoops, while a full tweed skirt worn with a cashmere sweater was just the ticket for the college-bound coed. With all these outfits, saddle shoes and white wool or cotton bobby sox provided finishing touches.

Highly popular were the pastel bouffant dresses with tops featuring spaghetti straps, which fell to just below the knee. These were worn with nylon stockings and matching, medium heels, giving a girl the same sort of silhouette as the plainer wool skirts did: wasp waist, wide skirt. Ideal for dreamy parties, bouffant skirts gave way to a sensible black wool jumper with a skirt underneath on less eventful days, or a plaid or gingham shirtwaist dress. More formal moments required a "little black dress," a must for any teenage girl's wardrobe during the 1950s.

The girls sported outerwear similar to that worn by women—that is, polo coats, car coats with detachable hoods, or short "toppers." Loose, bulky sweaters worn with high-waisted dungarees or, for somewhat less relaxed moments, tapered slacks or stretch pants were fine for cool autumn days.

For informal occasions, there were also tight black Capri pants that stopped six inches above the ankle; narrow, low-cut black flats reminiscent of ballet shoes; a tight, wide belt; and white (or, if one were frivolous enough, pink) blouse or top. White cotton Bermuda shorts and tailored shirts, or short shorts combined with sleeveless

and collarless tops were both worn with sandals come summer. Unlike the daring swimsuits featured in high-fashion magazines, however, most fifties teenage girls wore swimsuits that were cumbersome and unrevealing, with a little skirt or fabric panel to hide the crotch.

Hair was cut into short, curly "poodle" cuts or shaggier Italian cuts swept back into a ponytail (with or without a part), or it was teased into an elaborate bouffant that called for special one-and-three-quarter-inch-mesh rollers and was known to reach widths of fourteen inches. Costume jewelry was worn more frequently than the real thing.

As for makeup, once considered taboo for all but "tramps," fifties teenage girls went in for it in a big way. Lips were accentuated with lipstick (*the* cosmetic of the fifties: teenage girls spent a total of $20 million a year on it), available in a vast range of shades, including blue and black. Eyes were emphasized with mascara and lining pencil, all in coordinating hues (eyeshadow, however, was suitable only for post-teens). Fingernails were polished in shades of red or pink.

Although adults and the young people of the so-called Silent Generation did not dress alike, they dressed in the same spirit. Both groups avoided idiosyncratic clothes, preferring to blend in with and win the acceptance of their peers. In their favor, it can be said that boys' clothing was sturdy and girls' clothing inventive, if not always practical or easy to wear. Yet these clothes were also one more means by which the decade's conformism was reinforced. They served as a norm to which teenagers had to aspire or else be cast out from the group—a fate just a little bit worse than death in the other-directed fifties. Conservative and a bit drab and clunky-looking, these clothes give no hint of the vivid attire that would be ushered in by the youth revolution of the sixties, yet they served their purpose at the time. It is ironic, though, that today these very clothes are favored not by conservative young people but by a fashionable avant-garde, who are apt to see them as hilarous yet naive camp items.

Full-scale rebellion against fifties conformity was not to take place until the middle of the next decade. But even during the 1950s there were some young Americans who, dissatisfied with the status quo, made their presence known both in the way they dressed and in the way they behaved. True, most teenagers of the Silent Generation embraced consumerism with even more enthusiasm than their parents did. Yet at the same time, concern over juvenile delinquency rose sharply. It was not only the violence, vandal-

Johnny, the character Marlon Brando played in the 1953 movie *The Wild One,* that provided the most immediate inspiration for the greaser style, although its roots go back to both Nazi and Italian fascist garb as well as to the "Teddy Boy" proletarian look of postwar British teenagers. The idea was to look poor, tough, and hard—cold as ice, angry as hell, macho arrogant, and dressed to kill. The girlfriends who hung out with them were no pushovers, either, with their elaborately teased and sprayed hairdos, heavy

codes and forbid such aberrant apparel, at least within the precincts of school. The American Institute of Men's and Boys' Wear even waged a "dress right" campaign, with Francis deW. Pratt, president of that organization, declaring that, insofar as clothes went, "Men and boys must be sold on their economic and social importance. They must see that clothing helps them in business or in school. Then they will get interested in the details of their dress."

Of course, this campaign was no

The Young and the Restless

ism, and disrespect that alarmed solid citizens. The style in which those "hoody" teenagers dressed got to them, too.

In fact, the young and the restless had their uniform, just as the corporate executive did, only theirs was a lot sexier: skin-tight black jeans, black hobnail boots, black T-shirt or gray sweatshirt, and black leather motorcycle jacket. Boys' hair was worn long and elaborately styled into a greasy duck's tail á la rock 'n' roll idol Elvis Presley. But Elvis's soft side—his wholesome love of mom and the kind of innocence that led him to defend his teasing gyrations by saying "It's all leg movements. Ah don't do nothin' with my body"—held no appeal for greasers. The more extreme sartorial excesses of Elvis (gold lamé outfits and so on) and lesser-known rockers like Tony Conn (leopard-skin jackets with sequinned lapels and orange pants) scandalized adults, but these, too, went unemulated. Rather, it was

makeup, tight, hot pink sweaters, short skirts, stockings, and decided lack of a so-called feminine softness.

The greaser look was a violent one, but greasers and assorted "j.d."s were not the only fifties Americans given to brutality. Indeed, a fascination with violence held sway over many supposedly relaxed, happy, and optimistic Americans (particularly adult males) during the 1950s. They may not have been getting dressed up in leather and roaring into small, dull American towns on Triumphs, but they were devouring the bloody detective tales penned by Mickey Spillane, whose heroes, in their efforts to rid the land of commies, were as prone to brutality as any greaser. It was not these armchair vigilantes, however, who raised such a hue and cry; it was the more flashily dressed greasers and their girlfriends.

By the late 1950s, disapproval of their attire had reached such a pitch that the question arose as to whether high schools should institute dress

more than a ploy to get males to buy more clothes in a decade when, despite prosperity, the men's clothing industry was sagging (and a ploy, incidentally, which manufacturers of jeans and leather jackets were none too happy about). But the "dress right" slogan quickly acquired moral overtones. As an article in a 1958 issue of *Senior Scholastic* pointed out, the black-leather-jacket look "is associated in the public mind with criminals—and therefore has no place in school. The article continued, "Teenagers go to school to learn how to become better citizens... part of good citizenship is learning how to dress and act properly... being a bum is not being 'modern.'" Some, however, disagreed. The article went on to quote one Fred Sparks, a "nationally-syndicated columnist," who informed teachers that if they'd "'permit students to blow off steam on wacky wardrobes... they'll be less apt to talk about blowing up the government.'"

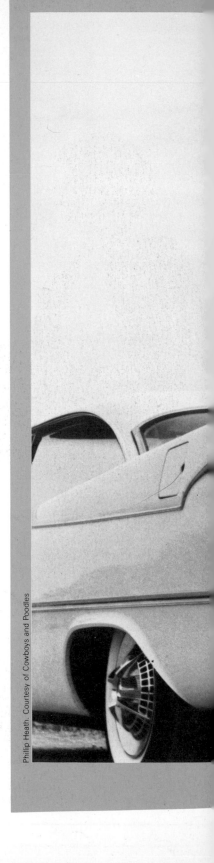

Phillip Heath. Courtesy of Cowboys and Poodles

There is no mistaking these people for inhabitants of the fifties, despite the clothes and the car. They look up at the sky too pessimistically to have come from that particular tract of time. (Pessimism aside, though, there's no doubt—these clothes are hot.)

The Kobal Collection

The Kobal Collection

Elvis Presley, like any teen idol, inspired distinct fashion looks. Here, he wears a sports jacket as no one else could.

The article closed with a defense of sturdy denim, though not of the sexier, more sinister black leather: ''President Eisenhower's grandson, David, has been photographed on his way to school—wearing blue jeans! Has anyone censured the President's family for fostering a potential 'troublemaker'?'' Still, some schools did adopt dress codes, and young ''troublemakers'' continued to irritate their elders.

A somewhat less irksome mode of anti-establishment attire was favored by a quieter, more artistically inclined and slightly older group of rebels: the beatniks. Like greasers, beats also favored black clothes. But while black for the former betokened evil, for the latter it expressed sensitivity. These people were seen in the flesh primarily in such cultural centers as New York and San Francisco (and were inspired

by the postwar Paris existentialist crowd)—he with his black turtleneck sweater, baggy trousers, beret, and beard; she with her long hair, hand-crafted leather sandals, black leotards, and dance skirt. People feared aggressive greasers. Contemplative, non-threatening beatniks, on the other hand, were ignored or considered fit subject for mockery. Ten years later, however, critics were not mocking but teaching Beat Generation master-pieces like Jack Kerouac's *On the Road*, Allen Ginsberg's ''Howl,'' and William S. Burroughs' *Naked Lunch* in university literature courses.

As Stuart and Elizabeth Ewen note in *Channels of Desire*, beatnik ''anti-fashion became a conspicuous weapon of outrage'' during the fifties—outrage at the conformity, rampant consumerism, and racism at

Grease, the movie version of the Broadway musical, starring John Travolta and Olivia Newton-John *(left)*, reflected the ever-growing fascination of today's under-30s with 1950s teen culture.

If sex and rage often must go hand in hand, it is no surprise that Marlon Brando's rage-filled Johnny in *The Wild Ones* presents such a potent sexual stereotype. Indeed, some people still find beat-up leather jackets like the one he wears *(right)* sexy.

home, and the Cold War politics and nuclear arms race abroad. Nevertheless, the fashion business assimilated the Beat spirit quickly—much more quickly, in fact, than did the academy, and despite its nonconformist connotations. By 1959, no less conformist a magazine than *Life* was featuring loose sweaters (including one in "gloomy maroon") and black slacks in its splashy fashion plates, one of which boasted real "male Beats, who wear standard garb that Beats consider to be in, [and]...look all flaked out." Like can you dig, daddy-o? Fifties America may well have been in need of dissenting voices (as well as dissenting clothing styles), but the United States would have to wait a decade for the hippies and student activists of the sixties, for social and political protest that could not be laughed off so easily.

The Kobal Collection

With its Republican president and politically conservative atmosphere, eighties America—at least the America of the early 1980s—resembles fifties America in some respects. And it is true that 1950s fashions are back in style again, particularly among urban and suburban youth ''into'' New Wave rock, who identify with the New Wave scene. But this fashion trend is fifties with a difference. Thirty years ago the Capri pants, cat's-eye sunglasses, and other 1950s regalia so voguish today were worn with no thought to campiness or rebellion. They had a certain casualness and peppiness about them that was thoroughly in keeping with American postwar optimism.

Today, however, many people—especially those under thirty—are not overly optimistic about the future. Nuclear nightmares haunted the popular imagination of the 1950s. Today they strike many people as a possible daytime threat—a reality rather than a dream. And so it is no wonder that fashionable young people don clothes recalling an era of nuclear naivete with a decidedly ironic air. They appreciate the absurdity of clothes whose frivolity, when seen in retrospect, implies total obliviousness on the part of the wearer to the events that brought World War II to its shocking, ominous end. If ever there was a time to harbor doubts about the future, it was in the immediate aftermath of Hiroshima. But American teenagers in the fifties were too busy shopping to wax apocalyptic (unlike, say, the beatniks, whose moody black sweaters might be ''read'' as symbols of existentialist despair)—and their clothes said as much.

Today's New Wave types like the ''fun'' aspects of 1950s clothes. The more excessive teen styles and screaming, frankly synthetic-looking hues carry the greatest appeal. But in the 1980s that notion of ''fun'' is dosed with an all-too-knowing cynicism. Young people may once have

All in Good Fun

Photographer Cindy Sherman plays a woman of the fifties world in her 1979 self-portrait, *Untitled Film Still*.

The zany patterns of Stewart Lucas's hand-painted ties *(left)* contain images of the television set he had been "glued to" for so many hours during the 1950s.

Today's young people embrace the fifties style with varying degrees of enthusiasm. The woman at left has dressed to an extreme, hanging out in that strapless party dress in front of a wildly souped-up fifties car parked by that hang-out of fifties hang-outs, the malt shoppe. The pensive young man *(above)* standing near the palm tree, on the other hand, favors a sporty, low-key fifties jacket, though his "attitude" seems rebellious.

won the admiration and acceptance of their peers thanks to these outfits. Now, when the American Dream seems more questionable than ever, the keeping-up-with-the-Joneses mentality in clothes as in other consumables strikes New Wavers as a laughable if not altogether pathetic response to blatant media manipulation. When New Wavers adopt fifties fashions or newer designs inspired by 1950s originals, they do so not so much to impress one another and conform with the group (though that is part of it) as to "outrage" one another, in a subculture where deadpan yet at the same time hilariously bizarre idiosyncrasy figures prominently in both wardrobe and "attitude." Curiously enough, despite the knowing, cynical air with which these clothes are worn, there actually is something authentically "fifties" about the outlook that goes with the clothes, informed as it is by the same political indifference that characterized the so-called 1950s Silent Generation. Now, of course, the indifference has a nihilistic tinge, a sense of disgust with politics. Back in the 1950s, most young people did not care enough to know that there was anything to be disgusted about.

Though it may express a certain cynicism, wearing fifties or fifties-style clothes in the 1980s can be interpreted as a kind of social protest in and of itself. To do so is to make a statement, one that mocks—sometimes affectionately, sometimes with more venom, depending on how exaggerated the clothes are—the values of the fifties, and to a certain extent those of the eighties, which Americans hold so dear. In addition to the statement, the clothes are also easy to wear. Inexpensive and often remarkably durable, originals can be bought at vintage clothes shops, sometimes for quite reasonable prices, and they never fail to bring a note of levity to a get-together. What's more, they offer a colorful alternative to today's bland "preppie" look, or the more expensive high-fashion look, both of which suggest a throwback (though not a very humorous or critical one) to the fifties — that most conservative of all the decades.

Bibliography

Allen, James Sloan. *The Romance of Commerce and Culture*. Chicago: The University of Chicago Press, 1983.

"The American Look." *Time*, 2 May 1955, 85.

Angelucci, Enzo. *Airplanes: From the Dawn of Flight to the Present Day*. New York: McGraw-Hill Book Co., 1971.

Annual Conference of American Craftsmen. Published transcripts. American Craftsmen's Council.

Art Direction. All issues, 1955–1959.

Art Directors Club Annual of Advertising Art. 1950–1959.

Baeder, John. *Diners*. New York: Harry N. Abrams, 1978.

Baines, Barbara Burman. *Fashion Revivals*. New York: Drama Book Publishers, 1981.

Banham, Rayner. "The Missing Motel." *Landscape* 15, no. 2 (Winter 1965–1966).

Batterberry, Michael and Ariane. *Fashion: The Mirror of History*. New York: Greenwich House, distributed by Crown Publishers, 1977.

Bell, Quentin. *On Human Finery*. New York: Schocken Books, 1976.

Black, J. Anderson, and Garland, Madge. *A History of Fashion*. New York: William Morrow & Co., 1975.

Blanchard, Fessenden. "Revolution in Clothes." *Harper's Magazine*, March 1953, 59–64.

Bony, Anne. *Les Années 50*. Paris: Éditions du Regard, 1982.

Booth-Clibborn, Edward, and Baroni, Daniele. *The Language of Graphics*. New York: Harry N. Abrams, 1974.

The Bowling Proprietor. All issues, 1957–1959.

Caplan, Ralph. *The Design of Herman Miller*. New York: Whitney Library of Design, Watson-Guptill Publications, 1976.

Chappell, Russell. "Male Animal: How to Get Him Dressed?" *Newsweek*, 30 December 1957, 52.

Clark, Garth, and Hughto, Margie. *A Century of Ceramics in the United States: 1878–1978*. New York: E.P. Dutton, 1979.

Constantine, Mildred, and Lenor Larsen, Jack. *Beyond Craft: The Art Fabric*. New York: Van Nostrand Reinhold Co., 1973.

Consumer Reports. All issues, 1956.

Cook, Jeffrey. *The Architecture of Bruce Goff*. New York: Harper & Row, 1978.

Corson, Richard. *Fashions in Hair*. London: Peter Owen, 1971.

Corson, Richard. *Fashions in Makeup*. New York: Universe Books, 1972.

Cosmopolitan. Special teen issue, November 1957.

Craft Horizons. All issues, 1950–1959.

Curtis, William J.R. *Modern Architecture Since 1900*. Englewood Cliffs, NJ: Prentice-Hall, 1982.

Darling, Sharon. *Chicago Furniture: Art, Craft & Industry: 1833–1983*. New York: The Chicago Historical Society in association with W.W. Norton & Co., 1984.

Design Quarterly. (Formerly *Everyday Art Quarterly: A Guide To Well Designed Products*.) Minneapolis, MN: Walker Art Center. All issues, 1950–1959.

Design Since 1945. Philadelphia Museum of Art, 1983.

Designer Craftsmen, U.S.A.—1953. Catalog of American Craftsmen's Educational Council exhibition.

The Detroit Institute of Arts, and The Metropolitan Museum of Art. *Design in America: The Cranbrook Vision, 1925–1950*. New York: Harry N. Abrams, 1983.

Doblin, Jay. *One Hundred Great Product Designs*. New York: Van Nostrand Reinhold Co., 1970.

Domergue, Denise. *Artists Design Furniture*. New York: Harry N. Abrams, 1984.

Dorothy Liebes. Catalog for Museum of Contemporary Crafts retrospective exhibition, 1970.

82 Distinctive Houses from Architectural Record. F.W. Dodge Corporation, 1952.

Ewen, Stuart and Elizabeth. *Channels of Desire*. New York: McGraw-Hill Book Co., 1982.

Ferebee Ann. *A History of Design from the Victorian Era to the Present*. New York: Van Nostrand Reinhold Co., 1970.

"50s Design—A Continuing Tradition." *Arts + Architecture* 2, no. 2. 1983.

Ford, Katherine Morrow, and Creighton, Thomas H. *Designs for Living*. New York: Reinhold Publishing Co., 1955.

Fraser, Antonia. *A History of Toys*. New York: Delacorte Press, 1966.

Furniture World. All issues, 1950–1952.

Gandy, Charles D., and Zimmermann-Stidham, Susan. *Contemporary Classics: Furniture of the Masters*. New York: McGraw-Hill Book Co., 1981.

The Gift and Art Buyer. All issues, 1953–1956.

Gluck, Felix, ed. *World Graphic Design*. New York: Watson-Guptill Publications, 1968.

Glynn, Prudence. *In Fashion*. New York: Oxford University Press, 1978.

Gomez, Linda. "The 10 Best & 10 Worst American Cars." *Life*, September 1983, 66-74.

Gowans, Alan. *Images of American Living: Four Centuries of Architecture and Furniture as Cultural Expression*. Philadelphia and New York: J.B. Lippincott Co., 1964.

Hall, Julie. *Tradition and Change: The New American Craftsman*. New York: E.P. Dutton, 1977.

Harper's Bazaar. All issues, 1950–1959.

Heimann, Jim, and Georges, Rip. *California Crazy: Roadside Vernacular Architecture*. San Francisco: Chronicle Books, 1980.

Henderson, Sally, and Landau, Robert. *Billboard Art*. San Francisco: Chronicle Books, 1980.

Hennessey, William J. *Modern Furnishings for the Home*. New York: Reinhold Publishing Co., 1952.

Hennessey, William J. *Russel Wright, American Designer*. Cambridge, MA: The MIT Press, 1983.

skett, John. *Industrial Design*. New York: Oxford University Press, 1980.

ke, Helen, and Pels, Walter. *The First Book of Toys*. New York: Franklin Watts, 1957.

rnung, Clarence P., and Johnson, Fridolf. *200 Years of American Graphic Art*. New York: George Braziller, 1976.

use & Garden. All issues, 1950–1959.

use + Home. All issues, 1952.

use Beautiful. All issues, 1950–1959.

dustrial Design. All issues, 1954–1959.

teriors. All issues, 1950–1959.

cobus, John. *Twentieth Century Architecture: The Middle Years 1940-65*. New York and Washington: Frederick A. Praeger, 1966.

ncks, Charles. *Modern Movements in Architecture*. Garden City, NY: Anchor Books, 1973.

zer, Marty, *The Dark Ages: Life in the United States 1945-1960*. Boston: South End Press, 1982.

atz, Sylvia. *Plastics: Designs and Materials*. London: Studio Vista, 1978.

atzenbach, Lois and William. *The Practical Book of American Wallpaper*. Philadelphia and New York: J.B. Lippincott Co., 1951.

unzle, David. *Fashion and Fetishism*. Totowa, NJ: Rowan and Littlefield, 1982.

apidus, Morris. *Architecture: A Profession and a Business*. New York: Reinhold Publishing Co., 1967.

arrabee, Eric, and Vignelli, Massimo. *Knoll Design*. New York: Harry N. Abrams, 1979.

ee, Sarah Tomerlin, ed. *American Fashion*. New York: Quadrangle/The New York Times Book Co., 1975.

fe. All isues, 1950–1959.

oewy, Raymond. *Industrial Design*. Woodstock, NY: The Overlook Press, 1979.

ucie-Smith, Edward. *A History of Industrial Design*. New York: Van Nostrand Reinhold Co., 1983.

urie, Alison. *The Language of Clothes*. New York: Vintage Books, 1983.

ynes, Russell. *The Tastemakers*. New York: Dover Publications, 1980.

Madigan, Mary Jean. *Steuben Glass*. New York: Harry N. Abrams, 1982.

Manchester, William. *The Glory and the Dream*. Toronto, New York, and London: Bantam Books, 1975.

Maurello, S. Ralph. *Commercial Art Techniques*. New York: Tudor Publishing Co., 1952.

McClintock, Inez and Marshall. *Toys in America*. Washington, DC: Public Affairs Press, 1961.

McCoy, Ester. *Craig Ellwood*. New York: Walker & Co., 1968.

McGraw-Hill Encyclopedia of Science & Technology. New York: McGraw-Hill Book Co., 1982.

Meggs, Philip B. *A History of Graphic Design*. New York: Van Nostrand Reinhold Co., 1983.

Melinkoff, Ellen. *What We Wore*. New York: Quill, 1984.

Merriam, Eve. *Figleaf*. Philadelphia and New York: J.B. Lippincott & Co., 1960.

Miller, Douglas T., and Nowak, Mario. *The Fifties: The Way We Really Were*. Garden City, NY: Doubleday & Co., 1977.

Munson, Kenneth. *Famous Aircraft of All Time*. Poole, Dorset: Blandford Press, 1976.

Muschamp, Herbert. *Man About Town: Frank Lloyd Wright in New York City*. Cambridge, MA: The MIT Press, 1983.

Nelson, George, ed. *Display*. New York: Whitney Publications, 1952.

Nelson, George, ed. *Living Spaces*. New York: Whitney Publications, 1952.

Nordness, Lee. *Objects: U.S.A.* New York: The Viking Press, 1970.

Pulos, Arthur J. *American Design Ethic*. Cambridge, MA: The MIT Press, 1983.

Rae, John B. *The American Automobile: A Brief History*. Chicago and London: The University of Chicago Press, 1965.

Rossbach, Ed. "The Glitter and Glamour of Dorothy Liebes." *American Craft* (December 1982/January 1983).

Russell, Douglas A. *Costume History and Style*. Englewood Cliffs, NJ: Prentice-Hall, 1983.

Sann, Paul. *Fads, Follies and Delusions of the American People*. New York: Crown Publishers, 1967.

Schoeffler, O.E., and Gale, William. *Esquire's Encyclopedia of 20th Century Men's Fashions*. New York McGraw-Hill Book Company, 1973.

Schreier, Barbara A. *Mystique and Identity: Women's Fashions of the 1950s*. Norfolk, VA: The Chrysler Museum, 1984.

Senior Scholastic. "Dress Codes...Cool or Square?" 21 November 1958.

Snibbe, Richard W. *Small Commercial Buildings*. New York: Reinhold Publishing Co., 1956.

Stern, Robert A.M., ed. "American Architecture: After Modernism." *A+U Architecture and Urbanism*, Special issue, March 1981.

Tafuri, Manfredo, and del Co, Francesco. *Modern Architecture*. New York: Harry N. Abrams, 1979.

Tourist Court Journal. All issues, 1957–1959.

Toys and Novelties. All issues, 1955–1959.

Trahey, Jane, ed. *Harper's Bazaar: 100 Years of the American Female*. New York: Random House, 1967.

Van Doren, Harold, *Industrial Design*. 2d ed. New York: McGraw-Hill Book Co., 1954.

Vieyra, Daniel R. *"Fill 'Er Up": An Architectural History of America's Gas Stations*. New York: Macmillan Publishing Co., 1979.

Vogue. All issues, 1950–1959.

Wallance, Don. *Shaping America's Products*. New York: Reinhold Publishing Co., 1956.

Walz, Barbara, and Morris, Bernardine. *The Fashion Makers*. New York: Random House, 1978.

Whiffen, Marcus, and Koeper, Frederick. *American Architecture, Vol. 2: 1869-1976*. Cambridge, MA: The MIT Press, 1983.

Wilcox, R. Turner. *Five Centuries of American Costume*. New York: Charles Scribner's Sons, 1963.

Wilcox, R. Turner. *The Mode in Costume*. New York: Charles Scribner's Sons, 1958.

Wildenhain, Marguerite. *Pottery: Form and Expression*. American Craftsmen's Council, 1959.

Wilson, Eunice. *A History of Shoe Fashions*. New York: Theatre Art Books, 1968.

Wolfe, Tom. *From Bauhaus to Our House*. New York: Pocket Books, 1982.

The World in Vogue. Compiled by The Viking Press and *Vogue*. New York: The Viking Press, 1963.

Wright, Gwendolyn. *Building the Dream*. New York: Pantheon Books, 1981.

Sources and Mail-Order Addresses

British and European Sources

Although most of the objects described in this book originated in America, many similar items are available in Europe. In addition, European designers of the fifties produced a wealth of material of their own, primarily influenced by the styles illustrated in this book.

With the revival of interest in the fifties, many shops specializing in art and design of this era have sprung up throughout Europe. Listed below is a selection of these.

UNITED KINGDOM

AMERICAN CLASSICS
400–404 Kings Road
London SW10
Tel: 01–352 2853

AMERICAN RETRO
13 Kensington Market
Kensington High Street
London W8
Tel: 01–937 9431

85 Kings Road
London SW3
Tel: 01–351 6616

ASTROHOME LTD
47 Neal Street
London WC2
Tel: 01–240 0420

BUTLER & WILSON
189 Fulham Road
London SW3
Tel: 01–352 3045

COBRA & BELLAMY
149 Sloane Street
London SW1
Tel: 01–730 2823

DETAIL
49 Endell Street
London WC2
Tel: 01–379 6940

THE FIFTIES WAREHOUSE
Unit 4, 58 Battersea High Street
London SW11
Tel: 01–350 0427

FLIP INTERNATIONAL LTD
125 Long Acre
London WC2
Tel: 01–836 7044

GRAYS MEWS ANTIQUE MARKET
1 Davies Mews
London W1
Tel: 01–629 7034

HYPER HYPER
26–40 Kensington High Street
London W8
Tel: 01–937 6501

JOHN JESSE & IRINA LASKI
160 Kensington Church Street
London W8
Tel: 01–229 0312

PINK SODA
57 Great Portland Street
London W1
Tel: 01–636 9001

PRACTICAL STYLING
Centre Point
16–18 St Giles High Street
London WC2
Tel: 01–240 3711

PRODUCTS
4–6 Northington Street
London WC1
Tel: 01–430 0660

PRUSKIN GALLERY
Chenil Galleries
Kings Road
London SW3
Tel: 01–351 2154

CHRISTOPHER STRANGEWAYS
19 The Market
Covent Garden
London WC2
Tel: 01–379 7675

3 Holland Street
London W8
Tel: 01–937 3251

THEMES & VARIATIONS
231 Westbourne Grove
London W11
Tel: 01–727 5531

In addition to the sources listed above in the U.K., you will find fifties originals and fifties-inspired products at most street markets.

CONTINENT OF EUROPE

DUC ET CAMROUX
56 rue Jean-Jacques Rousseau
75001 Paris
France

FIESTA GALERIE
103 rue du Cherche-Midi
75006 Paris
France

GALERIE 1800–2000
8 rue Bonaparte
75006 Paris
France

GALERIE LOFT
3 bis, rue des Beaux Arts
75006 Paris
France

MEMPHIS ARC 74
Corso Europa 2
Milan 20122
Italy

QUARTETT GALLERY
Knochenhauerstrasse 30
D–3000 Hanover 1
West Germany

Sources and Mail-Order Addresses

United States

Fifties-inspired Art

LEO CASTELLI
420 West Broadway
New York, NY

SIMONE GAD
4235½ Avocado St.
Los Angeles, CA

TRACEY GARET GALLERY
204 East 10th St.
New York, NY

GRACIE MANSION GALLERY
337 East 10th St.
New York, NY

METRO PICTURES
150 Greene St.
New York, NY

ROBERT MILLER GALLERY
724 Fifth Ave.
New York, NY

TONY SHAFRAZI GALLERY
163 Mercer St.
New York, NY

HOLLY SOLOMON GALLERY
724 Fifth Ave.
New York, NY

Fifties-inspired Products

EVANGELINE DECORATIVE ACCESSORIES
Box 309
Victoria Station
Montreal, Quebec CANADA

LEADWORKS INC.
3401 Richmond Rd.
Beachwood, OH

Fifties-inspired Crafts

CONVERGENCE GALLERY
484 Broome St.
New York, NY

HADLER-RODRIGUEZ GALLERY
38 East 57th St.
New York, NY

SNYDERMAN GALLERY
317 South St.
Philadelphia, PA

THE WORKS GALLERY
319 South St.
Philadelphia, PA

Fifties-inspired Designers/Architects

ARQUITECTONICA
4215 Ponce de Leon Blvd.
Coral Gables, FL

ALAN HESS
29 Belle Ave.
San Anselmo, CA

KRUECK & OLSEN, ARCHITECTS
213 West Institute Pl.
Chicago, IL

VINCUS MEILUS
38 Tiffany Pl.
Brooklyn, NY

PATINO/WOLF ASSOCIATES
400 East 52nd St.
New York, NY

VENTURI, RAUCH & SCOTT BROWN
4236 Main St.
Philadelphia, PA

Fifties-inspired Furniture and Furnishings

ARC INTERNATIONAL, INC.
476 Riverside Ave.
Jacksonville, FL

ATELIER INTERNATIONAL
595 Madison Ave.
New York, NY

CASTELLI FURNITURE INC.
950 Third Ave.
New York, NY

CONRAN'S
160 East 54th St.
New York, NY

FUN GALLERY
254 East 10th St.
New York, NY

I.D. INTERNATIONAL
979 Third Ave.
New York, NY

JENSEN-LEWIS CO., INC.
89 Seventh Ave.
New York, NY

PAUL LUDIK
333 East 5th St.
New York, NY

MICHAEL McDONOUGH
131 Spring St.
New York, NY

MODERN AGE
795 Broadway
New York, NY

THE RED STUDIO
301 Church St.
New York, NY

REMAINS
4990 Parker Ave.
Dept. I 10
St. Louis, MO

LARRY WHITELY GALLERY
111 North La Brea Ave.
Los Angeles, CA

Fifties-inspired Clothes

Many designers offer fifties-inspired designs. Their clothes are sold at hundreds of different clothing stores, most of which carry many outfits that are *not* fifties-inspired. The following list includes some of these designers or stores.

BETSEY JOHNSON
1441 Broadway
New York, NY

MODERN GIRLS AT PLAY
169 Thompson St.
New York, NY

NEIMAN MARCUS
Main & Evoy
Dallas, TX

Fifties Vintage Clothes

ANTIQUE BOUTIQUE
712–714 Broadway
New York, NY

Fifties Originals

In addition to the stores in the following list, Salvation Army thrift shops and Goodwill outlets are excellent and inexpensive sources of mass-produced fifties furniture.

Fifties Originals Still in Production

Index

About the Author

Cynthia Hill

RICHARD HORN is a novelist and journalist specializing in design and architecture. His articles have appeared in such publications as The Home Section of *The New York Times, Architectural Digest, New York, Art & Antiques, Metropolitan Home, Industrial Design,* and the Italian design magazines *Gran Bazaar* and *FMR.* He has also published *Memphis: Objects, Furniture, and Patterns* (1985) and *Designs* (1981), a playful *roman a clef* about the New York design scene. In collaboration with Billy Bergman, he has also written *Recombinant Do-Re-Mi,* a book about experimental pop music. A graduate of Columbia College and a Kellett Fellow, he is currently senior editor of *House Beautiful's Home Decorating.*